Nonfiction Strategies That Work

Teachers are being bombarded with ideas for teaching nonfiction, but what *really* works? In this essential book, dynamic author Lori G. Wilfong describes ten best practices for teaching nonfiction and how to implement them in the classroom. She also points out practices that should be avoided, helping you figure out which strategies to ditch and which to embrace.

Topics covered include . . .

- ♦ Finding quality, differentiated texts to teach content
- ♦ Selecting support strategies with purpose
- ♦ Providing students with a range of scaffolds for effective summary writing
- ♦ Purposely selecting vocabulary words to support content learning
- ♦ Working with students to develop strategies to cite textual evidence
- ♦ Using text structure as both a reading and writing tool for analyzing nonfiction
- ♦ And much more!

Every chapter begins with an engaging scenario and ends with action steps to help you get started. The book also contains tons of handy templates that you can reproduce and use in your own classroom.

Lori G. Wilfong is a former middle school language arts teacher, current Associate Professor in Middle Childhood Education at Kent State University, frequent conference presenter, and forever supporter of teachers working to weave literacy into their classrooms.

T0347517

Other Eye On Education Books Available from Routledge
(www.routledge.com/eyeoneducation)

Vocabulary Strategies That Work: Do This—Not That!
Lori G. Wilfong

Teaching the Common Core Speaking and Listening Standards:
Strategies and Digital Tools
Kristen Swanson

The Common Core Grammar Toolkit:
Using Mentor Texts to Teach the Language Standards in Grades 3–5
Sean Ruday

The Common Core Grammar Toolkit:
Using Mentor Texts to Teach the Language Standards in Grades 6–8
Sean Ruday

Authentic Learning Experiences:
A Real-World Approach to Project-Based Learning
Dayna Laur

Writing Behind Every Door:
Common Core Writing in the Content Areas
Heather Wolpert-Gawron

Rebuilding Research Writing:
Strategies for Sparking Informational Inquiry
Nanci Werner-Burke, Karin Knaus, and Amy Helt DeCamp

Flipping Your English Class to Reach All Learners:
Strategies and Lesson Plans
Troy Cockrum

Big Skills for the Common Core:
Literacy Strategies for the 6–12 Classroom
Amy Benjamin and Michael Hugelmeyer

Common Core Literacy Lesson Plans: Ready-to-Use Resources, K–5
Common Core Literacy Lesson Plans: Ready-to-Use Resources, 6–8
Common Core Literacy Lesson Plans: Ready-to-Use Resources, 9–12
Edited by Lauren Davis

Teaching Students to Dig Deeper:
The Common Core in Action
Ben Johnson

Nonfiction Strategies That Work

Do This—Not That!

Lori G. Wilfong

Routledge
Taylor & Francis Group

NEW YORK AND LONDON

First published 2014
by Routledge
711 Third Avenue, New York, NY 10017

and by Routledge
2 Park Square, Milton Park, Abingdon, Oxon OX14 4RN

Routledge is an imprint of the Taylor & Francis Group, an informa business

© 2014 Taylor & Francis

The right of Lori G. Wilfong to be identified as author of this work
has been asserted by her in accordance with sections 77 and 78 of the
Copyright, Designs and Patents Act 1988.

All rights reserved. No part of this book may be reprinted or
reproduced or utilized in any form or by any electronic, mechanical,
or other means, now known or hereafter invented, including
photocopying and recording, or in any information storage or
retrieval system, without permission in writing from the publishers.

Trademark notice: Product or corporate names may be trademarks
or registered trademarks, and are used only for identification and
explanation without intent to infringe.

Library of Congress Cataloging-in-Publication Data
Wilfong, Lori G.
Nonfiction strategies that work : do this—not that! / Lori G. Wilfong.
      pages cm
  1. Literature—Study and teaching (Elementary)   2. Prose literature—
Study and teaching (Elementary)   3. Reportage literature—Study and
teaching (Elementary)   I. Title.
   LB1575.W554 2014
   372.62′3—dc23
   2013044524

ISBN: 978-0-415-73528-5 (hbk)
ISBN: 978-0-415-72208-7 (pbk)
ISBN: 978-1-315-85849-4 (ebk)

Typeset in Palatino
by Apex CoVantage, LLC

For Bob, who only reads nonfiction.

For Bob, who only understands.

Contents

Setup of This Book

To describe each item on the **Do This—Not That** list, this text has been set up with a specific structure:

♦ A description of the research behind each "Do This" item

♦ Strategies that update traditional instructional practice for each item on the list

♦ Common Core State Standards that correlate with each strategy

♦ Action steps and reflection items for each item to help spur your instructional change!

Supplemental Downloads

Several of the tools featured in this book are also available for free download on our website, at www.routledge.com/books/details/9780415722087. Click on the tab that says Supplemental Downloads. Teachers can print and photocopy these tools for classroom use.

Meet the Author

Lori G. Wilfong, Ph.D., began her career as a naïve (and yet know-it-all) teacher at a middle school in East Los Angeles. Two days into her job teaching English to sixth, seventh, and eighth grade English Language Learners, she realized how much she didn't know about teaching and this set the course for the rest of her career: to learn as much as she could about motivating adolescent readers, reading in the content areas, young adult literature, and differentiated instruction. A frenzy of advanced degree getting followed, including a master's in Reading Specialization and a doctorate in Curriculum & Instruction, both from Kent State University. She worked as a literacy coach and a literacy specialist in rural and urban districts in Northeast Ohio before landing in the department of Teaching, Learning, and Curriculum Studies at Kent State University at Stark, where she currently is an Associate Professor, teaching courses in literacy to both preservice and practicing teachers.

Lori continues to hone her skills in school districts, working with teachers with one goal always in mind: to make all students love reading. Her first book, *Vocabulary Strategies That Work: Do This—Not That!*, was published in late 2012. She lives in Munroe Falls, Ohio, with her husband, Bob.

DO THIS!	NOT THAT . . .
1. Select and instruct support strategies with purpose	1. Simply assign readings without scaffolding or modeling effective reading strategies
2. Provide students with a range of scaffolds for effective summary writing	2. Assign a summary to be written without giving clear expectations
3. Go beyond the textbook to find quality, differentiated texts to teach content	3. Only derive reading assignments from a "one-size-fits-all" reading source
4. Purposefully select and study vocabulary words to support content learning	4. Rely on textbooks to dictate which words to teach
5. Work with content area colleagues to select nonfiction topics that cross the curriculum	5. Work in isolation on nonfiction topics
6. Work with students to develop strategies to cite evidence when working with all texts	6. Allow students to address text topics without being held accountable for using evidence
7. Create and scaffold varied and interesting writing assignments that range from informal to formal, depending on purpose	7. Assign one or two major writing projects throughout the year with little time for the writing process to occur
8. Use text structure as both a reading and writing tool to assist students in analyzing any nonfiction text	8. Teach text structure in isolation
9. Encourage independent reading of nonfiction texts as part of a balanced self-selected reading diet	9. Read nonfiction texts only in whole group settings
10. Use nonfiction for active comprehension strategies like Readers' Theatre, and Tableaux	10. Make nonfiction reading a passive, seated experience only

Take a look at your nonfiction teaching practices in language arts, and based on the list, record the following:

Things I am doing now that need to be updated:	Instructional updates I can use:

Brainstorm: What evidence can you provide to show that you are changing your instructional practice in the teaching of nonfiction text in language arts?

_____

_____

_____

_____

_____

_____

_____

_____

_____

_____

_____

_____

_____

Introduction

Do this—not that! sums up my philosophy of professional development for teachers in a nutshell. I found that all the professional development I went through as a teacher and, later, the professional development I delivered as a literacy consultant and professor, centered on the hottest trends in instructional strategies. This was great—except I was never quite sure what strategies I was currently using that I needed to cease. So instead, I would experience that feeling of being totally overwhelmed, maybe try out a new strategy once or twice, and then revert back to my original ways. Sound familiar?

This type of professional development is what inspired the first book in the *Do This—Not That!* series. An administrator in a district that I worked closely with wanted to help teachers spring clean their vocabulary practices. We developed a list of new strategies and theories for them to apply to their teaching AND we paired the list with the strategies and theories that had become outdated that they needed to stop using. Teachers had a clear picture of what needed to be updated, and why, and what they could use to replace their traditional teaching methods.

When thinking about the next topic to tackle in this manner, the use of nonfiction text for language arts teachers was a no-brainer. Identified as one of the key shifts in implementing the Common Core State Standards, many teachers panicked at the idea of revamping their language arts curriculum to include nonfiction reading and writing in authentic and engaging ways. This text was written to calm those fears—nonfiction can be great!

Enjoy the process of updating your nonfiction instructional practices!

Chapter 1

Select and Instruct Nonfiction Support Strategies with Purpose

"How does your teaching of nonfiction differ from your instruction of fiction texts?" I asked the group of fifth grade teachers sitting in front of me. A look of guilt crossed their faces. One teacher raised a timid hand in the back. "To be honest," she said, "we usually just skip those stories in the textbook. The kids find them boring." The other teachers around her nodded their heads in agreement. Another teacher raised her hand, more boldly this time. "I think you can't go wrong with a good ol' KWL chart." A few more heads bobbed to bless this strategy. I wrote KWL on the dry erase board behind me. "Anything else?" I asked, hoping that the KWL strategy might open a flood of other nonfiction strategies. Judging from the lack of eye contact from the group, I knew we were done.

Why Is This Item on the List So Important?

It is no secret that the Common Core State Standards have brought to light an interesting paradox in the teaching of language arts: we teach reading, but the majority of the reading we teach is fiction. When the revised standards were released, an equal amount of attention was finally given to the teaching of nonfiction texts; 10 standards devoted to the comprehension, vocabulary, author's craft, and analysis of informational pieces. And the language arts world was thrown into a bit of a tizzy. Appendix A of the Common Core Standards (CCSS, 2011) clearly states that the type of reading students do should change—50% nonfiction texts in grades three through five, 70% nonfiction texts in grades six through eight, and 80% nonfiction texts in grades nine through twelve. It is easy to brush this recommendation off, thinking that our content area colleagues will come to bail us out. And it is true: our content area colleagues are now charged with their own literacy standards for use in their classrooms. But as the primary teacher of reading and writing, our responsibility to prepare students to effectively comprehend and respond to all texts, especially nonfiction, is greater than ever.

A portion of this responsibility lies in the strategies we use in our classroom to ease our students into reading nonfiction. These strategies can be twists on traditional fiction reading strategies but they also can be tailored to suit the unique characteristics of nonfiction text—examination of headings and captions, for example. In any case, we need a specific set of strategies that will scaffold independent reading of these texts so that students can end the year feeling ready to tackle any text with confidence:

> **Do this—not that principle #1:** DO select and instruct support strategies with purpose; DON'T simply assign readings without scaffolding or modeling effective reading strategies.

Instructional Practices to Update

Updated Strategy #1: Read Nonfiction like Fiction

Thomas Newkirk (2012) states, "We crave narrative." It is simply in our human nature to look for problem and solutions, storylines, *plot,* in all reading, not just what we think of as typical fiction. So it makes sense to help students see the narrative in all texts—what problem does the text present? Who are the characters (and these are not always people in nonfiction text!)? How is the problem solved? By helping students see that a nonfiction text does not mean abandoning everything they already know about reading (mostly from fiction texts), we are alleviating some of the anxiety that nonfiction texts produce.

To use this strategy, you will want to begin with a nonfiction text that has all the elements of narrative. Newspaper or gossip magazine articles are a great place to start. Here is an article excerpted from www.timeforkids. com (a favorite source for kid-aimed news articles—more about that in Chapter 3):

Twins For the Record

Eleven-year-old twins Luke and Ryan Novosel of Wilmette, Illinois, had a goal. The fifth-graders wanted to set a Guinness world record. Some of their friends had already tried to jump on a pogo stick longer than anyone else. One even attempted to produce the loudest burp. But none of them came close.

This article has all the elements of a great narrative—characters, a problem, and the beginning of a plot. It can be broken down into the elements on the Nonfiction to Narrative template (Figure 1.1):

Figure 1.1   Nonfiction to Narrative Template

Title of text _____ Twins for the Record _____

Players of importance _____ Luke and Ryan Novosel _____

Setting _____ Wilmette, IL _____

Aha!
Moment

Problem – No one was even getting close
They weren't

Solution

Background information

Ending

The twins wanted to set a world record

If we keep reading, we are able to identify more elements of the narrative unfolding:

Then Luke and Ryan realized that there were lots of other twins in their grade at Highcrest Middle School. They did a full count, and were amazed to discover 24 sets of twins in all. Most of them are fraternal, or non-identical. Of those 24 sets, three are boy-boy, 11 are girl-girl, and 10 are boy-girl. There are only two pairs of identical twins—all girls.

"We were absolutely shocked," Luke and Ryan's mother, Nancy Fendley, told the Associated Press. The boys figured they now had their Guinness record: most pairs of twins in one grade. The current record is 16 pairs, and is shared by Valley Southwoods Freshman High School in Iowa, Staples High School in Connecticut, and Maine South High School in Illinois.

Proving the Point

Earlier this year, Luke and Ryan—with help from their parents—sent an application to Guinness. They added birth certificates, photos, and proof that all of the sets of twins attend Highcrest Middle School. They expect to hear back in several weeks on whether they actually set a new world record.

"The whole school thinks it's the greatest thing," Fendley said. "It's been such a fun, creative experience."

Figure 1.2 Completed Nonfiction to Narrative Template

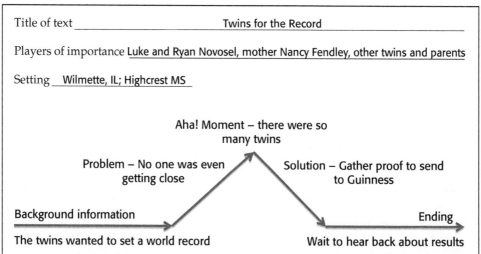

As long as the article is not to purely inform (many encyclopedia entries fit this category), most nonfiction text fits this template—even textbooks!

Figure 1.3 is an excerpt of an eighth grade history textbook, which perfectly fits the Nonfiction to Narrative template.

Figure 1.3 Nonfiction to Narrative—Eighth Grade Social Studies Example

---

The Battle of Shiloh

General Grant and about 40,000 troops then headed south along the Tennessee River toward Corinth, Mississippi, an important railroad junction. In early April 1862, the Union army camped at Pittsburg Landing, 20 miles from Corinth. Nearby was a church named Shiloh. Additional Union forces came from Nashville to join Grant.

Confederate leaders decided to strike first, before the reinforcements arrived. Early in the morning of April 6, Confederate forces led by Albert Sidney Johnston and P.G.T. Beauregard launched a surprise attack on the Union troops. The **Battle of Shiloh** lasted two days, with some of the most bitter, bloody fighting of the war. The first day, the Confederates drove Grant and his troops back to the Tennessee River. The second day, the Union forces recovered. Aided by the 25,000 troops from Nashville and shelling by gunboats on the river, they defeated the Confederates, who withdrew to Corinth.

(American Journey, 2012)

It is easy to pick out the narrative elements, as seen in Figure 1.4 (a blank template is included at the end of the chapter).

Figure 1.4 Nonfiction to Narrative Template—The Battle of Shiloh

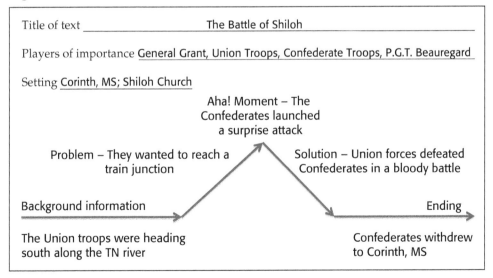

Updated Strategy #2: Selecting Appropriate Pre-During-Post
Supports for Nonfiction Texts

The KWL mentioned in the anecdote in the beginning of the chapter is there for a reason: KWLs work. The simple organization of helping students figure out what they already know about a topic before they begin reading, what they want to learn from the reading, and the place to record what they did learn is a structural tool that will never go out of fashion (Ogle, 1986).

The structure of the KWL lends itself nicely to a variety of strategies that support students before, during, and after they read. There are many great texts out there written solely about these strategies including, *50 Instructional Routines to Develop Content Literacy* (Fisher, Brozo, Frey, & Ivey, 2010) and *Classroom Strategies for Interactive Reading* (Buehl, 2008). The strategies presented here fall into my "greatest hits" collection—they are engaging and meaningful and provide direct connections to Common Core Informational Text Standards.

I am a big believer of using routines to support learning for all students, and comprehension strategies, like the ones described below, fall neatly into a reading routine across content areas. If a grade level team can agree on a set number of strategies to use for a quarter, semester, or even a year—say three pre, three during, and three post strategies—then they will have 27 different ways they can teach any text! Each teacher can select one pre, one during, and one post strategy to use with the text and mix it up depending on the text being taught. And once the strategies are initially taught (usually by the language arts teacher), the teacher can focus on making the meaning of the text come alive. Table 1.1 lists the pre, during, and postreading strategies described in this section; more of these strategies are described throughout the book (Chapters 2, 4, 5, 8, and 10 have strategies that can be added to Table 1.1).

Table 1.1 Pre, During, and Postreading Strategies

PRE	DURING	POST
Tea Party	Sketch to Stretch	I Am Poems
Book Box	Text Annotations	License Plates

Prereading strategies. Prereading strategies have come under fire under the Common Core. David Coleman, an architect of the Common Core State Standards for English Language Arts, has very clearly stated that prereading activities can cloud student judgment and "free" them of doing the work required when actually reading the text (Coleman, 2011). In some ways, his logic is correct; we spend so much time on the prereading portion of a text that by the time it comes to actually *read* the text, students don't need to read it because we have already informed them what the text is about. A good prereading strategy should pique interest and set questions for reading but not give away anything. Most importantly, it should be quick; the strategies described here are all five minutes or less to get student brains rolling in the right direction, essentially warming them up for reading. I actually like to use a swimming pool analogy when discussing prereading strategies—do you jump into a pool without dipping your toe in first? Very few of us do. But, with a toe here and an arm there, we ease ourselves in. That is what prereading strategies do—they help us ease into reading.

Tea Party (Wilhelm, 2002). Tea Parties are a great way to introduce students to a new text without fear of over-teaching. Directions:

1. Preview the text to be read. Write or type important sentences on strips of paper. Make one for each student in the classroom (each strip does not need to have a new sentence; sentences can be repeated).

2. On the day the text is to be read, distribute one strip per student (I distribute these very purposefully to ensure that all students can participate with dignity, i.e., shorter sentences to students who struggle with reading aloud or are new to the English language).

3. Give a short amount of time (30 seconds suffices) for students to read their strip to themselves several times. Walk around to support students with unknown vocabulary.

4. Model the strategy: Keep a strip for yourself and walk up to a student. Read your strip aloud clearly and slowly and then invite the student to read back to you. Remind students that they can only say to each other what is on their strips of paper.

5. IMPORTANT—model "pondering" the conversation. The purpose of this strategy is for students to preview the text. If they don't stop after reading their strip with another student and think about how their sentence might connect with their peer's sentence, then it simply is an exercise in fluency (an auxiliary benefit but not the one we really want!).

6. Invite students to get up and participate in the Tea Party, reading aloud their strip to as many different students as possible, pausing to listen to their peers read back to them and ponder the connections. Three minutes is generally more than enough time for students to mingle at the Tea Party. Make sure you mingle as well with your strip, to ensure that students stay on task.

7. When three minutes is up, invite students to return to their seats and chat with an elbow buddy about the "gossip" at the Tea Party.

8. Finally, invite students to get out the text in question and begin reading.

Book Box (Jonson, 2006). Book Boxes entice students to reading with the trick of building suspense. You can do a Book Box in two distinct ways but they each start with the same steps:

1. Preview the text to be read. Select four symbols/items that will help generate interest in the text.

   a. Book Box variation #1: Fill an actual box or bag with the items brainstormed in #1. Before reading the text, pull the items out of the box or bag and remind students that these items all relate to the text about to be read.

   b. Book Box variation #2: Create a PowerPoint or document, using clip art or images to represent the items brainstormed in #1. Print these out for students and pass them out or display them on an overhead. Figure 1.5 shows an example of a PowerPoint Book Box for John Brown's Final Speech to the Court.

2. After reading the text, have students return to the Book Box and relate the items to the text.

Figure 1.5 Book Box Sample–John Brown's Final Speech to the Court

During reading strategies. As adults, many of us admit to reading a text, getting to the bottom of the page, and realizing that we have no idea what it is we just read. This is metacognition in action: thinking about our thinking (and then going back and reading again to actually learn something). It takes proficient readers a lot of practice and self-awareness to realize that they are not doing a good job comprehending a text, and, for students new to a text or a type of text, this issue can be magnified. This is where during reading strategies are helpful; they help a student to focus while reading, really paying attention to what is going on in a text and noting important information.

I recently gave an article to a group of teachers to read during a professional development session and then sat back and watched what they did to help focus themselves during reading. Several dug highlighters out of their bags and marked the important information, while others used a pen or pencil to underline what interested or stood out to them. A final group wrote notes to themselves in the margin, anything from questions to ask during our discussion to agreements and exclamations with statements from the text. After they read (and before they discussed the article), I asked them to divulge where these strategies came from. Their answers were not surprising: "I learned to do that in college," said a highlighter. "It helps me focus on important information," continued an underliner. "It makes me feel like I am having a conversation with the author," admitted a margin writer, seeming embarrassed with this confession. I then asked them if their students had these same strategies. The margin writer answered with an emphatic, "No. If I tell them to underline or highlight important information, they underline or highlight everything. And I can't have them write in the margins because most of our informational text is in a textbook."

Intentional teaching of during reading strategies helps students to develop their own methods for helping them concentrate during reading. Eventually, these strategies can simply be reminders to students to use when necessary to help them concentrate while reading any text.

Sketch to Stretch (McLaughlin & Allen, 2002; Rasinski & Padak, 2000; Wilfong, 2012). Marzano (2010) makes an engaging plea for translating text into pictures—he contends it is how we remember our lives and therefore a great strategy for helping a student recall important information from a text. Donna Wilson (2012) calls this making "brain movies," where our comprehension in a text lies in our ability to take information and translate, or code, the text into visuals. Sketch to Stretch capitalizes on this use of pictures to recall textual information by helping students stop to consider what information a section of text presents, translating that information into a picture drawn by the student, and then continuing through following sections in the same manner. The stop/start nature of this strategy mirrors the popular "Chunk and Chew" method described by Kryza, Duncan, and Stephens (2009), who believe that managing instruction and reading by allowing students to stop and process information at regular intervals improves comprehension in all students.

To introduce Sketch to Stretch, I like to start with a picture book or engaging text that I can read aloud to students. I later scaffold the strategy onto more traditional prose like an article or textbook.

1. Preview the text to be read, designating clear stopping points.

2. Distribute blank paper to students and have them fold the paper into eight boxes (elementary school teachers have taught me to do the hot dog fold first and then a hamburger fold—when you open it up, you have four boxes on each side). To make life easy, you can also just distribute a sheet with a four box table on it.

3. Explain to students that you will read the text aloud. When you stop, you will give them two minutes to sketch what they think is the most important piece of information from what you just read. Reinforce the idea that two minutes is quick and that you do *not* expect Rembrants or Picassos.

4. Read aloud and come to the first stopping point. Model your think aloud process for students: what was most important about what you just read? Sketch quickly (and poorly, so that they see it is truly not about the quality of the sketch). Add a caption or word bubble, if necessary.

5. Continue to the next stopping point. Guide practice by allowing a student to suggest what should be drawn next to capture the important information from that section of the text.

6. Continue on, pausing to allow students to sketch.

7. When the text is finished, students have created a graphic novel/cartoon of the important information from the text and are able to use it to guide a retell or a summary, or as textual evidence for further writing.

A few things to keep in mind with this strategy—two minutes can be too much time! Adjust the time as necessary, especially as students get accustomed to sketching. When students are ready, present an article in a Sketch to Stretch format, with boxes opposite text to show students where they should stop and reflect on the information, as shown in Figure 1.6.

Figure 1.6   Sample Sketch to Stretch Text Set-up for Scaffolded Practice

Text	Sketch
France, the largest country in Western Europe, has long been a gateway between the continent's northern and southern regions. Its lengthy borders touch Germany and Belgium in the north; the Atlantic Ocean in the west; the Pyrenees Mountains and Spain in the south. Wide fertile plains dominate most of the north and west, making France the agricultural epicenter of Europe. The sprawling, forested plateau of the Massif Central, a range of ancient mountains and extinct volcanoes, occupies France's southern interior.	

Excerpt from http://kids.nationalgeographic.com/kids/places/find/france/, 2013

Finally, as students master the concept, you simply remind them that Sketch to Stretch is a strategy they can use as they wish to help them concentrate while reading. I personally think of the strategy as a precursor to taking notes in books in college and will often bring in a textbook or two to demonstrate that marking up the text is neither welcomed nor encouraged, until they start buying the book! Until students own the book, I keep piles of sticky notes and colored paper available for them to use with this strategy.

Text Annotations (Hoch, Bernhardt, Murphy-Schiller, & Fisher, 2013; Vaughn & Estes, 1986). Text annotation is exactly what the teacher at the beginning of the "During Reading Strategies" section was doing when she said that she writes in the margins because it was "like having a conversation with the author." If we dive further in the cognitive process, she was making the internal thinking that we have with a text explicit by noting her actual thinking on the text—questioning the author, responses to important or interesting information, and more (Hoch et al., 2013). Proficient readers come to this strategy naturally; they automatically are having a conversation with the text and the author, and usually all it takes is a teacher inviting them to write on the text to get them started on this lifelong habit of many good readers. Struggling readers need more than just an invitation to mark up the text; they need a teacher to show them a specific manner of text annotation that they can take ownership of and adapt to their own needs. This is one such system.

1. First, introduce students to a set system of text annotation. Figure 1.7 shows one example of text annotations.

2. On a classroom digital display, put up a sample text. Model for students the think aloud process, reading the text aloud and inserting the appropriate symbols, to show your reactions to the text in the first few paragraphs. Make sure you share your reasons for using specific symbols.

3. Distribute the text to students. Read the next few paragraphs together, allowing students to raise their hands and show when they are using the text annotation symbols and to explain why they are using them.

4. Allow students to continue reading, using the text annotation system as appropriate.

5. After reading, students can gather in small groups and discuss the text, using their annotations to share reactions and ideas after reading.

Figure 1.7   Sample Text Annotations (adapted from Vaughn & Estes, 1986)

✓	I agree
?	I have a question
??	I don't understand
✗	I disagree
+	This is new information
!	Cool fact!
✪	This is important

As students become comfortable with either Sketch to Stretch or Text Annotations, they can have the freedom to choose these or other during reading strategies to help them stay focused while reading any text.

Postreading strategies. It only makes sense that after reading a text, you respond. Chapters 2 and 7 contain ideas for summarizing and writing in response to texts; the two strategies presented here allow students to creatively show what they learned from a text.

Postreading strategies need to go beyond simple questions that students answer at the end of a passage. I often prompt preservice and practicing teachers alike to re-examine Bloom's Taxonomy (1956) and think how they can assist their students in doing more than just basic recall; challenging them to evaluate, synthesize, and apply.

The two strategies presented here could be used with fiction or nonfiction, alike; however, when used with informational text, they allow a student to use the same type of creativity that we often associate with fiction text with an informative one.

I Am Poem. Tell students that after they read a text they are going to write a poem about it, and it is possible that they will run screaming the other way (try it, just for fun!). The great thing about the I Am poem is that it provides a scaffold for poetry writing about any topic that ensures success and differentiation for all.

1. Before instruction, fill in an I Am poem template about yourself to use during modeling (my own sample, abbreviated I Am poem is in Figure 1.8; a blank template is at the end of the chapter).

Figure 1.8 Sample I Am Poem

I am <u>Lori Wilfong</u>.
I wonder <u>why the Cleveland Browns don't win more football games.</u>
I hear <u>my husband yelling at the TV when they miss a scoring opportunity.</u>
I see <u>the remote go flying in his frustration.</u>
I want <u>the Browns to win more games.</u>
I am <u>Lori Wilfong</u>.

2. Show students your model, explaining that I Am poems are as simple as filling in the blanks appropriately.
3. As a class, select a common topic to write a poem about together. Choose an inanimate object to write about to show that the I Am poem is about more than people (the school building is a popular choice during this practice). Fill out a blank template together, guiding practice.
4. Allow students to create their own I Am poem about themselves (great getting to know you activity!).
5. Read a piece of informational text. Brainstorm with students the different perspectives that are present in the piece. Figure 1.9 is a sample informational text article to use with this strategy, excerpted from Time For Kids (Abrams, 2013).
6. Pass out a blank I Am poem template. Allow students to select a perspective from the article and complete the template from that perspective. Remind students about inference; we might not know why an astronaut cries but we can infer this information based on the text and our own background knowledge. Figure 1.10 is a sample I Am poem from the perspective of Valentina Tershkova, the first woman in space.

Figure 1.9   Sample Informational Text Article for Use with I Am Poem Template

Women Flying High

Fifty years ago this week, Russian cosmonaut Valentina Tereshkova made history by becoming the first woman in space. Since then, other women have followed the trail she blazed—and more are on the way. On Monday, NASA, the U.S. space agency, selected eight new astronauts—half of them female. This is NASA's first new class of astronauts in four years, and it features the agency's highest-ever percentage of women.

Shooting for the Stars

Tereshkova flew into space on June 16, 1963, on the three-day Vostok 6 mission. It took place just two years after another Russian cosmonaut, Yuri Gagarin, achieved the first piloted spaceflight in 1961.

A textile worker from a modest family, Tereshkova became interested in parachuting at a young age. Her experience in parachute jumping led to her being recruited as a cosmonaut by the Russian government. Tereshkova and four other women were part of the first all-female cosmonaut training group in 1961, but only Tereshkova ever completed a flight.

Tereshkova became an instant celebrity upon returning to Earth. She has received many awards and honors since her flight. Today, she serves in the Russian government.

Looking Ahead

After Tereshkova's landmark mission, it would take another 20 years for the United States to send a woman into space. Astronaut Sally Ride became the first female American astronaut to leave Earth on June 18, 1983. Since then, a total of 57 women from nine different countries have blasted off.

Two women are currently in orbit. NASA astronaut Karen Nyberg is aboard the International Space Station. Last week, China sent its second-ever female astronaut, Wang Yaping, to work on its orbiting space module. However, Tereshkova remains the only woman to complete a solo flight.

In recent years, NASA has run into trouble with funding. Currently, there are no American spacecraft that can carry humans to space. However, this new class of astronaut candidates suggests that NASA is looking ahead to the future of space exploration. The group includes the first female fighter pilot to become an astronaut in almost two decades, as well as a female helicopter pilot.

The class will begin training in August. "They're excited about the science we're doing on the International Space Station and our plan to . . . [go] there on spacecraft built by American companies," said NASA Administrator Charles Bolden in a statement. "And they're ready to help lead the first human mission to an asteroid and then on to Mars."

Excerpted from Time For Kids (Abrams, 2013)

Figure 1.10 Sample I Am Poem Based on "Women Flying High"

I am <u>Valentina Tereshkova.</u>

I wonder <u>how my family felt when I decided to leave the textile industry for parachuting.</u>

I hear <u>people say that I was breaking barriers for women everywhere.</u>

I see <u>the stars and planets from my shuttle.</u>

I want <u>more women to follow in my footsteps.</u>

I am <u>Valentina Tereshkova.</u>

The ease of the strategy allows it to be what I call "naturally differentiated." There are two more stanzas, in addition to the ones used in the samples, allowing students ready to write more to do so. The lines allow students to write a lot or a little, depending on their development. Making it text based allows for students to show that they understood the reading; some teachers do like to make a requirement for the number of lines that should reflect textual evidence so that students are doing more than just making inferences.

One of my favorite ways to wrap up use of the I Am poem is to have the students share them in a two-voice poem style. Have students find a partner who wrote his or her poem from a different perspective. Tell them to select a stanza and to practice reading it with one student saying a line from his or her point of view, followed by the other student. I find that these two voice poems become magical; even though students didn't write together, the simple fact that they were based on the same text means that their thoughts will mirror each other. It validates their comprehension and poem writing abilities in one!

Final word on I Am poems—they are definitely not limited to just historical figures or characters. One of the best versions of the I Am poem that I have seen was done in a math class. It is included for your enjoyment in Figure 1.11.

Figure 1.11 Math I Am Poem

I am <u>the decimal point.</u>

I wonder <u>if the student will put me in the right place.</u>

I hear <u>the student trying to figure out where I go.</u>

I see <u>numbers on either side of me.</u>

I want <u>to be in the right place.</u>

I am <u>the decimal point.</u>

Personalized License Plates. True confession: I have had several personalized license plates. Growing up in Southern California, vanity plates were simply a way of expressing who you were in the car that you spent so much time in because of the traffic.

Personalized License Plate #1: TODNZR

This personalized plate was chosen to reflect my obsession with ballet at the age of 16.

Personalized License Plate #2: CAJYHK

This personalized plate was chosen to show how I was a Californian attending the University of Kansas.

Personalized License Plate #3: CADRMN

This personalized plate was one I planned on getting upon moving to Ohio to reflect my longing for the sunny California weather (but it turns out I love Ohio).

All three of my personal plates reflect, or summarize, who I was at that time in my life. It is a fun way to allow students to show comprehension of a topic or text.

Lesson One:

1. Brainstorm your own personalized license plate, reflecting who you are as a person.
2. Post your license plate for students to puzzle through. Resource: Templates of all state license plates can be found and used at www.imagechef.com/c/6jjo/License-Plates.
3. Explain to students that personalized license plates are a reflection of a topic or feeling. For guided practice, select a topic of interest together (sports figures are popular choices) and brainstorm in small groups the possible personalized license plates for that topic.
4. Finish teaching the strategy by allowing students to create a personalized license plate for themselves.

Lesson Two:

1. Select an informational text to read.
2. Have students read the text and then brainstorm the different topics that could have a personalized license plate from the reading. Using the text from Figure 1.9, you could pick the various astronauts discussed, a country, or even the space station!
3. Have students created personalized license plate(s) for one or more of the topics. Make it clear that simply shortening a name (*a la* text language) does not show comprehension of a text. An example of

this would be the first woman in space, Valentina Tereshkova. Many students would try to make a personalized license plate that reads VLTNA but that does nothing but show her name. A more creative, and comprehension worthy, license plate might read 1WMNSPC.

A few rules to keep in mind: most license plates have seven or eight letters (check for your state). In California, some symbols are available for use in license plates including a heart, arrow, eye, and star.

As with the I Am poem, some of the best license plates I have seen have been on content area topics. One teacher assigned her students different triangles (which they had been studying in math) and asked them to create personalized license plates based on the attributes. A girl who was assigned an acute triangle made a license plate that read ANGLS90. At first, we argued with her that in an acute triangle, the angles were less than 90, but she eloquently argued back: "If you read it carefully you would see that I expect the reader to reuse the LS in ANGLS so that it read 'Angles less than 90.'" Indeed.

Common Core Connection

The strategies presented above fit well with a variety of standards in the Common Core State Standards for English Language Arts. They are presented in Figure 1.12.

Figure 1.12 Common Core State Standards Addressed in this Chapter

Grade Level	4	5	6
Standard Addressed	**Reading Standards for Informational Text** Refer to details and examples in a text when explaining what the text says explicitly and when drawing inferences from the text. Explain events, procedures, ideas, or concepts in a historical, scientific, or technical text, including what happened and why, based on specific information in the text. By the end of the year, read and comprehend informational texts.	**Reading Standards for Informational Text** Quote accurately when explaining what the text says explicitly and when drawing inferences. Explain the relationships or interactions between two or more individuals, events, ideas or concepts in a historical, scientific, or technical text based on specific information in the text. By the end of the year, read and comprehend informational texts.	**Reading Standards for Informational Text** Cite textual evidence to support analysis of what the text says explicitly as well as inferences drawn from the text. Analyze in detail how a key individual, event, or idea is introduced, illustrated, and elaborated in a text (e.g., through examples or anecdotes). By the end of the year, read and comprehend informational texts.

Grade Level	7	8	9–10
Standard Addressed	**Reading Standards for Informational Text** Cite several pieces of textual evidence to support analysis of what the text says explicitly as well as inferences drawn from the text. By the end of the year, read and comprehend informational texts.	**Reading Standards for Informational Text** Cite several pieces of textual evidence to support analysis of what the text says explicitly as well as inferences drawn from the text. By the end of the year, read and comprehend informational texts.	**Reading Standards for Informational Text** Cite strong and thorough textual evidence to support analysis of what the text says explicitly as well as inferences drawn from the text. Analyze how the author unfolds an analysis or series of events, including the order in which the points are made, how they are introduced and developed, and the connections drawn between them. By the end of the year, read and comprehend informational texts.

Action Steps

This chapter has introduced the idea of helping students see the narrative in nonfiction and how to focus and comprehend all informational texts. It is time to take some action:

1. Find a text to use in conjunction with the Nonfiction to Narrative template. After reading, have students work in groups to identify the narrative elements of the text using the template. Afterwards, ask students to reflect on the strategy. Did it help them break down the informational text? Why or why not? Record their answers here:

_____

_____

_____

_____

_____

2. Design a pre, during, post lesson to use with an informational text, choosing strategies from the six described in this chapter. After teaching the lesson, reflect on the process:

   a. Three strategies chosen: Pre _____ During _____ Post_____

   b. Did you enjoy planning in this format? Why or why not?

   _____

   _____

   c. Could you gauge the students' comprehension of the text from the postreading strategy you used?

   _____

   _____

   _____

Works Cited

Abrams, A. (2013, June). Women flying high. *Time for Kids*. Retrieved from www.timeforkids.com/news/women-flying-high/96531

Bloom, B. (1956). *Taxonomy of educational objectives, handbook I: The cognitive domain*. New York: David McKay Co.

Buehl, D. (2008). *Classroom strategies for interactive learning*. Newark, DE: International Reading Association.

Coleman, D. (2011). *Bringing the Common Core to life*. Presentation at the State Education Building, Albany, New York, April 28, 2011. Retrieved on December 11, 2013, http://usny.nysed.gov/rttt/docs/bringingthecommoncoretolife/part6transcript.pdf

Fisher, D., Brozo, W., Frey, N., & Ivey, G. (2010). *50 instructional routines to develop content literacy*. New York: Pearson.

Hoch, M., Bernhardt, R., Murphy-Schiller, M., & Fisher, J. (2013). Three important words: Students choose vocabulary to build comprehension of informational text. *Illinois Reading Council Journal, 41*, 3–12.

Jonson, K. (2006). *60 strategies for improving reading comprehension, K-8*. Thousand Oaks, CA: Corwin Press.

Kryza, K., Duncan, A., & Stephens, S. (2009). *Differentiation for real classrooms*. Thousand Oaks, CA: Corwin Press.

Marzano, R. (2010). Representing knowledge nonlinguistically. *Educational Leadership, 67*, 84–86.

McLaughlin, M., & Allen, M. (2002). *Guiding comprehension: A teaching model for grades 3–8*. Newark, DE: International Reading Association.

National Governors Association for Best Practices, Council of Chief State School Officers. (2011). Common core state standards (English language arts). Washington, DC: Author.

Newkirk, T. (2012). How we really comprehend nonfiction. *Educational Leadership, 69,* 28–32.

Ogle, D. (1986). K-W-L: A teaching model that develops active reading of expository text. *The Reading Teacher, 39,* 564–570.

Rasinski, T., & Padak N. (2000). *Effective reading strategies* (2nd ed.). Upper Saddle River, NJ: Prentice Hall.

Vaughn, J., & Estes, T. (1986). *Reading and reasoning beyond the primary grades.* Boston: Allyn & Bacon.

Wilfong, L. G. (2012). *Do this, not that! An eye on updating your vocabulary practices, grades 4–9.* New York: Routledge.

Wilhelm, J. (2002). *Action strategies for deepening comprehension: Using drama strategies to assist reading performance.* New York: Scholastic.

Wilson, D. (2012). Training the mind's eye: "Brain Movies" support comprehension and recall. *The Reading Teacher, 66,* 189–194.

Template 1.1   Nonfiction to Narrative Template

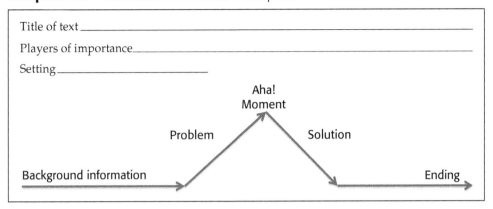

Title of text _____

Players of importance _____

Setting _____

Aha!
Moment

Problem   Solution

Background information   Ending

Copyright 2014 Taylor & Francis. All rights reserved. www.routledge.com

Template 1.2   Text Annotation Symbols

✓	I agree
?	I have a question
??	I don't understand
✕	I disagree
+	This is new information
!	Cool fact!
✪	This is important

Copyright 2014 Taylor & Francis. All rights reserved. www.routledge.com

Template 1.3   I Am Poem Template

I am _____

I wonder _____

I hear _____

I see _____

I want _____

I am _____

I pretend _____

I feel _____

I touch _____

I worry _____

I cry _____

I am _____

I understand _____

I say _____

I dream _____

I try _____

I hope _____

I am _____

Copyright 2014 Taylor & Francis. All rights reserved. www.routledge.com

Chapter 2

Provide Students with a Range of Scaffolds for Effective Summary Writing

Chandra looked up from the notecard she was holding, pausing to take a long breath. "Um, Chandra," I prompted her, looking at the clock, "how much longer is this summary of your book going to take?" She flipped the card over and examined her tiny writing. "Probably another five minutes, Mrs. W.," she replied. "A summary is all the important stuff you said, right?" I nodded back at her. "Well, there was a lot of important stuff because it was a long article."

Why Is This Item on the List So Important?

Chandra quite clearly articulated the problem with teaching summary to our students—we can give them a definition (in my case, it was "include the important stuff"), and then students will interpret that as they see fit. But summary writing is more than including pertinent information in a paragraph—it is an end product of student comprehension that is filled with cognitive processes: reading, deciding what information to keep and what information to discard, and figuring out how to take the "keep" information and restate it in a cohesive manner. Summary writing is a generative learning tool (BouJaoude & Tamim, 2008), assisting students to wrap up what they have learned in a neat package for later recall.

Summary writing is truly at the heart of nonfiction reading. We read nonfiction text primarily to learn new information and without the ability to summarize what we have learned, our takeaway from the reading, we are left with a jumble of facts and ideas that are difficult to make sense with (Dollins, 2012). The National Association of Employers and Colleges (2013) lists the ability to "obtain and process" information effectively as the number five most desired skill for college graduates. The ability to summarize falls into that skill set.

> Do this—not that principle #2: DO provide students with a range of scaffolds for effective summary writing. DON'T simply assign a summary to be written over a reading without giving clear expectations.

To Get Started

The techniques to scaffold summaries fall into three categories: summary frames, graphic organizers, and in-text techniques. All three work in the same manner by helping students narrow down information presented into a manageable format. However, I have found in my own teaching that one size does not fit all—different students are attracted to different techniques for a variety of reasons; some students find that a summarizing scaffold is more of a hinder than a help! In order to achieve our goal of helping all students learn how to summarize effectively, we must show them several strategies, modeled, guided, and used independently, so that eventually, students can select and apply a scaffold as he or she sees fit!

An instructional plan needs to be put into place—a time for the different scaffolds to be introduced and practiced, a rubric for summaries to be evaluated against (by both students and teachers!), and then a release of responsibility when students select and use a summarizing scaffold as the year progresses when necessary. There is no magic timetable for this; each teacher will need to evaluate how quickly to progress through the summarizing strategies before arriving at a place of independence. In any case, it will be helpful for students to keep models of this summarizing journey (perhaps in a readers' notebook) and to have templates enlarged and posted on walls as reminders as they progress through more difficult readings.

Although readability will be addressed in a later chapter, it is important with any new strategy to help scaffold success. I have to think about my purpose in teaching a strategy: In the beginning, it is not about learning new content but rather about mastering a skill (in this instance, summarizing). As the student begins to master the technique, the difficulty of the text can be amped up so that students can see if this scaffold is appropriate for their own independent reading and writing. I will often start a new strategy by selecting a palatable text, like a fiction picture book, and then select more difficult, nonfiction texts for later application. Figure 2.1 has a list of my favorite picture books to use with students to scaffold summarizing strategies.

Figure 2.1 My Top 5 Favorite Picture Books to Scaffold Great Summaries

1 *The Frog Prince Continued*, Jon Scieszka (1994)
2 *The True Story of the 3 Little Pigs*, Jon Scieszka (1996)
3 *This is Not My Hat*, Jon Klassen (2013)
4 *Smoky Night*, Eve Bunting (1999)
5 *Grandfather's Journey*, Allan Say (1994)

A basic rubric, shared across content areas, can be a great way to clarify expectations of what needs to be included in a summary. The ability to summarize is an anchor standard in the Common Core State Standards for Reading and Literacy Standards in History/Social Studies, Science, and Technical Subjects (number two), and the word "summarize" is actually used in the grade level standards beginning in grade 4. Figure 2.2 presents a sample rubric, developed by a seventh grade team of teachers in Maple Heights City Schools in Northeast Ohio, to be used in language arts, math, science, and social studies, so that they shared the same expectations for summary writing across content areas. You will notice three of the five categories are summary related (paraphrasing, content, and main idea), one category relates to language use (a value that all teachers shared and wanted to reiterate across content areas), and the top category asked students to write a more professional, rather than personal, summary, eliminating the use of the word "I" (stemming from a recurrence of the opening sentence, "I think the article was about . . .").

Figure 2.2 Common Core State Standards Based Summary Rubric

	2	**1**	**0**
No personal reference	No personal reference anywhere in the summary	One personal reference in the summary	Several personal references or opinions are present throughout the summary
Mechanics—spelling, grammar, and punctuation	This summary is mechanically perfect—there are no errors in spelling, grammar, or punctuation	This summary is getting there—there are a few spelling, grammar, and punctuation errors	There are so many mechanical errors in this summary that it detracts from its overall meaning
Paraphrasing	Text is summarized in student's own words	Text is mostly in student's own words; a few phrases are copied directly from text	Summary is copied directly from text; no original work is present in the summary
Content	Summary shows a complete understanding of the entire text	Summary shows understanding of part of the text	Summary does not show understanding of the text
Main idea	Most important point(s) of the text is included in summary	N/A	Most important point(s) of the text is not included in summary

Instructional Practices to Update

Updated Strategy #1: Summarizing Text Using Writing Frames

Writing frames are a scaffold themselves; they allow students to borrow the academic language necessary to complete a particular type of writing in a supported manner (Fisher & Frey, 2008; Wilfong, 2012). Several writing frames exist to support different types of writing: cause and effect, argument/persuasion, and, of course, summary writing.

A popular writing frame for summarizing is *The Important Book*, by Margaret Wise Brown (1949). The author of the popular children's book *Goodnight, Moon,* Brown unknowingly invented a summary frame with *The Important Book*. Each two-page spread is a summary of a different object: daisies, rain, a spoon, etc. The summary of each object follows the same pattern, shown in template form in Figure 2.3 (a full-size template is included at the end of the chapter).

Figure 2.3   The Most Important Thing About . . . Template

The most important thing about _____ is _____ .
It _____ .
It _____ .
And it _____ .
It _____ .
But, the most important thing about _____ is _____ .

Adapted from Dollins, 2012

This summary writing frame has two strengths: It presents the format of a paragraph with an introductory sentence ("The most important thing about . . ."), four supporting details, and a concluding sentence ("But, the most important thing about . . ."), and it helps separate out the main idea (first and last sentences) from supporting details (four middle sentences).

Identifying the main idea of a text is often the most difficult point when it comes to breaking down information into a summary. A student has to figure out the author's main intention in writing the text and that is not easy to do! I told Chandra, in the anecdote at the beginning of the chapter, that a summary was the important "stuff"; this strategy takes it a step further by prompting students to think what is *the* most important thing about whatever it is they are learning about.

To model this strategy, just like with the I Am poem from Chapter 1, I have students write about themselves first (another great "get to know you" idea to use in conjunction with a nonfiction text technique!). Students fill out the writing frame, substituting "I" for "It" (see Figure 2.3) and filling in their first names in the first blank of the first and last sentence. Be sure to prompt students to think hard about what is truly *the* most important thing about them and then to choose supporting details that relate back to that opening sentence.

For guided practice, select a descriptive text to use to help scaffold the writing frame (a more in depth discussion of text structure in the teaching of nonfiction takes place in Chapter 8). News articles, science and social studies textbooks, and Gail Gibbons' awesome nonfiction books (*Dinosaur Discoveries, Ducks, Nature's Green Umbrella*) all work great in conjunction with this strategy. Figure 2.4 contains an excerpt from *National Geographic Kids* that could be used to move students from a personal application of this summarizing technique to a text application.

Figure 2.4   Excerpt from *National Geographic Kids* to Use with "The Most Important Thing" Strategy

There are about 5,000 different species of ladybugs in the world. These much-loved critters are also known as lady beetles or ladybird beetles. They come in many different colors and patterns, but the most familiar in North America is the seven-spotted ladybug, with its shiny, red-and-black body.

In many cultures, ladybugs are considered good luck. Most people like them because they are pretty, graceful, and harmless to humans. But farmers love them because they eat aphids and other plant-eating pests. One ladybug can eat up to 5,000 insects in its lifetime!

Most ladybugs have oval, dome-shaped bodies with six short legs. Depending on the species, they can have spots, stripes, or no markings at all. Seven-spotted ladybugs are red or orange with three spots on each side and one in the middle. They have a black head with white patches on either side.

Source: National Geographic Kids, 2013

Students can work together to figure out which of these facts is *the* most important fact about ladybugs and select supporting details to use to fill in the remainder of the frame. Do remind students that the first and the last sentence are mirrors of each other; that is why choosing a truly important thing about the topic is imperative!

As students mature, the language of *The Important Book* may not seem appropriate. Working with a group of ninth grade students, we came up with four different ways to rephrase the opening sentence to sound like more sophisticated writers:

1. An important fact about _____ is

   _____.

2. Did you know that _____ is/was/were

   _____?

3. _____ have/had the ability to

   _____.

4. When studying _____, it is important to

   note_____.

To rephrase the closing sentence, we brainstormed these possibilities:

1. In conclusion, _____ are

   _____.

2. A/The _____ significance is solidified by the

   fact that _____.

3. This helps the reader understand that _____.

As students played around with the ideas above, they began to see the possibilities in writing summaries, as long as they worked within the confines of the The Most Important Thing template: a main idea, supporting details, and limiting themselves to the most important things.

The summary writing frame presented in this section can truly be applied across the curriculum. As a formative assessment, it can be completed at the end of a lesson to inform the instructor on what a student learned. After reading a section, chapter, or even after completing a unit, students can fill out the template to summarize learning in a concise manner. And, as intended, students can fill it out after reading a nonfiction text to help them break down a piece of text into the most important idea learned and its supporting details.

Updated Strategy #2: Summarizing Text Using Graphic Organizers

Using graphic organizers to make sense of reading texts has long been documented as effective (Kim, Vaughn, Wanzek, & Wei, 2004). Students use the format of the graphic organizer to help them search for important ideas in the text and place them in the appropriate spot on the page. A few basic graphic organizers for summary include the ubiquitous web:

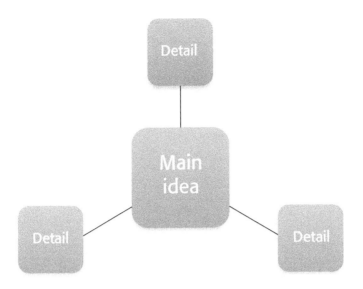

As students read, similar to The Important Thing About template, they fill in the boxes with the main idea and details of the text. Unlike the The Most Important Thing template, it doesn't ease the writing of the paragraph, itself. Students may struggle getting the information from the graphic organizer into an actual paragraph.

Another often-used graphic organizer for summary writing is the herringbone or fishbone:

Students write the main idea of the text on the center line (or the backbone) of the graphic organizer and put supporting details on the supporting lines (or bones).

Both of these graphic organizers are traditional for organizing summaries, and, for many students, they simply work. Students who do not need heavy scaffolding have the ability to subtract out the necessary information and use these types of graphic organizers for organization. However, for many students, especially as they struggle with the structure and ideas nonfiction text present, a little more heavy-lifting can be just the thing for writing great summaries.

In 1991, the International Reading Association published a brief text describing 10 ways that students could respond to literature. Included was the graphic organizer entitled Somebody Wanted But So Then (MacOn, Bewell, & Vogt, 1991). Originally conceived as a way to help students analyze conflict and resolution in fiction texts, it has since been applied to a variety of text types, including nonfiction (Beers, 2002). Like The Most Important Thing, it helps students break down a text into its components for use in summary writing. Figure 2.5 shows a blank template of the Somebody Wanted But So Then (SWBST) graphic organizer.

Figure 2.5   Somebody Wanted But So Then Graphic Organizer

Somebody	Wanted	But	So	Then

Unlike the graphic organizers presented above, SWBST asks the student to look for specific information in a text with a conflict and resolution. While this may seem confined to fiction texts, many great nonfiction narratives (news stories, historical narratives, biographies, and autobiographies) have conflict and resolution imbedded in the text, making them perfect for scaffolding summaries when teaching nonfiction. However, to introduce the strategy, I usually go back to a basic fairytale so that students can master the concept without struggling with a text. Figure 2.6 shows the SWBST strategy using the fairytale Cinderella.

Figure 2.6   SWBST Using Cinderella

Somebody	Wanted	But	So	Then
Cinderella	to go to the ball.	her evil stepmother and stepsisters forbade her to attend.	her fairy godmother came to her rescue and provided her with all she needed to attend.	she danced with Prince Charming at the ball, they fell in love, and lived happily ever after.

Using Figure 2.6, I am able to show students how they can take what we wrote in the graphic organizer and, with some strategic punctuation, turn it into a cohesive paragraph, using the headings of each column:

Cinderella (somebody) wanted to go to the ball (Columns 1 & 2). But, her evil stepmother and stepsisters forbade her to attend (Column 3). So, her fairy godmother came to her rescue and provided her with all she needed to attend (Column 4). Then, she danced with Prince Charming at the ball, they fell in love, and lived happily ever after (Column 5).

One of my favorite things about introducing this particular strategy to students is that I can challenge them to name any news or sports story and see if they are able to stump me in filling out the graphic organizer. Living in Northeast Ohio, the sports story of LeBron James leaving the Cleveland Cavaliers was (and still is) a big deal. A middle school student recently challenged me to work his leaving and winning two championships into a summary using SWBST (see Figure 2.7).

Figure 2.7

Somebody	Wanted	But	So	Then
Lebron James	to leave Cleveland in his quest to win a championship.	the Cavs did all they could to keep him, including offering him top dollar to stay.	he still took his talents to South Beach.	he won two championships with his new team and the Cavs are still not very good.

In many nonfiction texts, "something" not "someone" is the main idea. In this case, the column names can be tweaked to reflect the text needs:

Something	Is	But	So	Then/Now

After reading a news article about a world summit on global warming, students filled out the graphic organizer like this:

Something	Is	But	So	Then/Now
Global warming	a controversial scientific theory.	scientists have facts to prove its existence.	they held a summit to discuss the issues with world leaders.	world leaders are working together to solve these environmental issues.

One of the keys to using this graphic organizer is ensuring that the text has a conflict and at least the suggestion of a resolution. As students become more proficient at reading and recognizing different text structures, they should become adept at picking which scaffold to use when writing a summary.

Updated Strategy #3: Summarizing Text Using In-text Techniques

The final subset of summary scaffolds is using in-text techniques to help students select the important terms or ideas presented in a text and use them to write a summary. Rhoder (2002) presented a version of this strategy that many people are familiar with called GIST (as in, get the gist?). Students use the technique to identify the important term or idea in a particular paragraph or section of the text, transfer the idea from the text being read to a graphic organizer, and then use these terms or phrases to write a summary. The basic premise works beautifully; however, I found that many of my reluctant readers and writers didn't want to find information in a text and transfer it *anywhere*. They were ready for what I call in-text techniques to scaffold a summary—using the text itself as the jumping off point for writing.

This strategy is called "10 Words or Less." Ten is a totally arbitrary number; as the instructor, you can raise or lower the number of words you use for this strategy to appropriately match the text being read. As always, I start by modeling the strategy on the individual students:

1. Pass out 10 sticky notes to each student (or notecards, or a sheet with 10 boxes, or even simply have students rip a piece of paper into 10 pieces).

2. Model for students writing one word that describes yourself on each piece of paper. These words can be their place in life (brother, sister, daughter, son, student, athlete), adjectives (quiet, shy, loud, crazy), hobbies (knitter, swimmer), or anything else school appropriate. (Figure 2.8 shows my personal 10 words or less example; note the places I use phrases—each word counts as one—no cheating!)

3. Tell students to arrange their words any way they see fit; many students make categories, with personal attributes in one pile and labels in another. Others make a ranking from most to least important.

4. Have students turn to an elbow-buddy and tell them about themselves, using their 10 words and their set-up as a guide.

5. Finally, have students use their 10 words to write a summary of themselves.

Figure 2.8   Personal 10 Words or Less Example

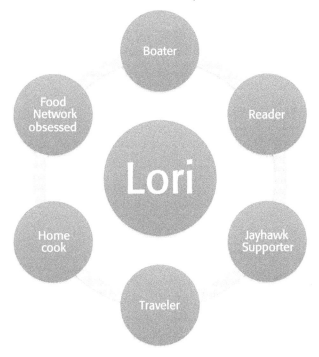

After the exercise described above, I explain (and often surprise) students by saying that summaries of text read can be written using the same strategy. Using a nonfiction text (no specific text structure needed here to make this strategy work), I guide practice by reading through an article together. I tell them we can only underline 10 words in the article. So, after reading through it once, we go back and nominate words for underlining. (Hint: There is always one student who wants to nominate "the" because "it shows up so much in the text." Silence them with one of your patented teacher stares.) At this juncture, students have the backbone of their summary: the 10 most important words/phrases of the text.

Have students take out a piece of paper and write the 10 words or phrases at the top. Then, have them flip the text over, pass it on, whatever you need to do to get it out of their hands. This is my safeguard against copying; one of the biggest complaints I get from teachers after reading student summaries is how much of the students' writing is plagiarized. Many students don't see the difference between plagiarizing/copying and summarizing; this strategy helps to break them of any bad habits they have developed. After students have handed back the text, they use their 10 words to craft a summary. For kinesthetic students, I have found that they like the manipulation of words on paper, like we did in the modeling step. For these students, I have piles of scratch paper available, where they can write each word or phrase and manipulate the order in which they want them to appear in their summary. Figure 2.9 shows a student example of the 10 words subtracted from the ladybug text in Figure 2.4 and the summary the student wrote from those 10 words.

Figure 2.9   Student Summary Example, Using 10 Words or Less

Ten words: Seven-spotted luck species red black dome eats aphids pests

Summary:
Many people think that the seven-spotted ladybug is good luck. This may because this red and black, dome-shaped bug eats aphids and pests.

Common Core Connection

As stated earlier, the Common Core State Standards begin including the word "summary" in Grade 4, Reading Informational Text, as well as in the Literacy Standards for History/Social Studies, Science, and Technical Subjects, beginning in Grade 6. Figure 2.10 presents these standards by grade level.

Figure 2.10   Common Core State Standards Addressed in this Chapter

Grade Level	4	5	6
Standard Addressed	**Reading Standards for Informational Text** Determine the main idea of a text and how it is supported by key details; summarize the text.	**Reading Standards for Informational Text** Determine two or more main ideas of a text and explain how they are supported by key details; summarize the text.	**Reading Standards for Informational Text** Determine a central idea of a text and how it is conveyed through particular details; provide a summary of the text distinct from personal opinions or judgments.

Grade Level	7	8	9–10
Standard Addressed	**Reading Standards for Informational Text** Determine two or more central ideas in a text and analyze their development over the course of the text; provide an objective summary of the text.	**Reading Standards for Informational Text** Determine a central idea of a text and analyze its development over the course of the text, including its relationship to supporting ideas; provide an objective summary of the text.	**Reading Standards for Informational Text** Determine a central idea of a text and analyze its development over the course of the text, including how it emerges and is shaped and refined by specific details; provide an objective summary of the text.
Grade Level	11–12		
Standards Addressed	**Reading Standards for Informational Text** Determine two or more central ideas of a text and analyze their development over the course of the text, including how they interact and build on one another to provide a complex analysis; provide an objective summary of the text.	**Reading Standards for Social Studies/History** Determine the central ideas or information of a primary or secondary source; provide an accurate summary of how key events or ideas develop over the course of the text.	**Reading Standards for Science & Technical Subjects** Determine the central ideas or conclusions of a text; trace the text's explanation or depiction of a complex process, phenomenon, or concept; provide an accurate summary of the text.

Action Steps

Scaffolding excellent summaries using nonfiction text is a challenge for teachers to undertake with their students. It is time to take some action:

1. Introducing the summary strategies presented in this chapter to students takes a bit of advanced planning. List, in order, the strategies that you will present to your students:

    a. _____

    b. _____

    c. _____

Why did you put them in that order?

_____

_____

_____

2. The Most Important Thing About writing frame and the SWBST graphic organizer require a specific type of text to scaffold good summaries (descriptive and conflict/resolution, respectfully). Find one of each text type to use with these summary strategies. List your sources here:

   a. Descriptive nonfiction text:

   _____

   b. Conflict/resolution nonfiction text:

   _____

3. Challenge: After you have introduced all three types of summary strategies, allow students to choose their scaffold as they see fit. Which type do most of your students gravitate toward? Why do you think that is?

_____

_____

_____

_____

Works Cited

BouJaoude, S., & Tamim, R. (2008). Middle school students' perceptions of the instructional value of analogies, summaries and answering questions in life science. *Science Educator, 17*, 72–78.

Beers, K. (2002). *When kids can't read—what teachers can do: A guide for teachers 6–12.* Portsmouth, NH: Heinemann.

Brown, M. W. (1949). *The important book.* New York: HarperCollins.

Dollins, C. (2012). Comprehending expository texts: Scaffolding students through writing summaries. *The California Reader, 45*, 22–28.

Fisher, D., & Frey, N. (2008). *Word wise and content rich, grades 7–12.* Portsmouth, NH: Heinemann.

Kim, A-H., Vaughn, S., Wanzek, J., & Wei, S. (2004). Graphic organizers and their effects on the reading comprehension of students with LD: A synthesis of research. *Journal of Learning Disabilities, 37*, 105–118.

MacOn, J., Bewell, D., & Vogt, M. (1991). *Responses to literature.* Newark, DE: International Reading Association.

National Association for Employers and Colleges. (2013). Employers rate candidate skills/qualities in order of importance (infographic). Retrieved July 15, 2013, from www.naceweb.org/infographics/employers-rate-candidate-skills-qualities.aspx

National Geographic Society. (2013). Creature features: Ladybugs. *National Geographic Kids.* Retrieved December 11, 2013, from http://kids.nationalgeographic.com/kids/animals/creaturefeature/ladybug/

Rhoder, C. (2002). Mindful reading: Strategy training that facilitates transfer. *Journal of Adolescent & Adult Literacy, 45,* 498–512.

Wilfong, L. (2012). *Vocabulary strategies that work: Do this—not that!* New York: Routledge.

Template 2.1   The Most Important Thing About

The most important thing about _____ is _____ .

It _____ .

It _____ .

And it _____ .

It _____ .

But, the most important thing about _____ is _____ .

Make it more sophisticated:

- An important fact about _____ is _____ .
- Did you know that _____ is/was/were _____ ?
- _____ have/had the ability to _____ .
- When studying _____ , it is important to note _____ .
- In conclusion, _____ are _____ .
- A/The _____ significance is solidified by the fact that

_____ .

Copyright 2014 Taylor & Francis. All rights reserved. www.routledge.com

Template 2.2   Somebody/Something Wanted/Is But So Then/Now

Somebody/Something	Wanted/Is	But	So	Then/Now

Write your summary in paragraph form here. It should have four sentences
(Column 1 & 2 = first sentence; Columns 3–5 = one sentence each):

_____

_____

_____

_____

_____

_____

Copyright 2014 Taylor & Francis. All rights reserved. www.routledge.com

Implement Quality, Differentiated Nonfiction Texts to Teach Language Arts Standards

As the teachers went through their curriculum maps, writing down the titles that they wished to keep that correlated with a particular standard and those they wished to discard, it became quickly apparent that there were not many, if any, nonfiction titles on either side of the list. Discussion took place amongst grade levels, favoring or dismissing certain books and short stories, sometimes accompanied by cries of "But I love that book!" or "I am so glad to get rid of that one." The fifth grade team reached the end of the process and called me over. "We are done!" one teacher proclaimed, spreading her hands to show me the work they had accomplished. But before I could respond, a teacher countered: "We are done with this part. But if you look at our list, you will see that we have almost no nonfiction titles. Lori, didn't you say we needed to try and get our nonfiction texts to comprise more than 60% of the texts we read with our students to get at the informational text standards?" I nodded in response and she turned back to the group, "We are just getting started."

Why Is This Item on the List So Important?

Scenes like the one described above are happening all over as schools work to meet the call for more nonfiction in the Common Core State Standards (CCSS). In fact, most current language arts state standards only have a 30% alignment with the CCSS, causing many school systems to scramble to up the rigor and complexity of texts read, while pulling in loads more nonfiction so that teachers feel capable in teaching the 10 Informational Text standards to their students (Porter, McMaken, Hwang, & Yang, 2011).

Let's be blunt: This is difficult. Many of us (and I include myself) became language arts teachers because a certain novel or author made us love literature and reading (in my case, Laurie Halse Anderson's *Speak,* encountered during my first young adult literature class as an undergraduate at the University of Kansas). We did not become language arts teachers because we loved "distinguishing claims that are supported by reasons and evidence from claims that are not" (CCSS, grade six, RI, #8). We know we need to change our paradigm. The CCSS asks us to assist students in achieving these standards with a variety of texts and text types, not specifically in *The Great Gatsby* or *Hatchet* (although we could use these texts to achieve these goals). But if you ask most English/ language arts teachers about their curriculum, they will name book titles, not standards or content: "This is my *Animal Farm* unit"; not "This is my argumentative reading unit." And that brings us back to the scramble to put mastery of standards first, no matter what text we are using. I have even developed a song about standards-based learning, called "Standards-Based Girl." Please feel free to sing the lyrics below to the tune of Madonna's song, "Material Girl":

> Some folks love them
> Some folks hate them
> Most think they're okay
> But the thing that we all know
> Is they're not going away
> (Chorus)
> 'Cause we are living in a standards-based world
> And I am a standards-based girl
> Ya' know,
> That we are living in a standards-based world
> And I am a standards-based girl

> **Do this—not that principle #3: DO implement quality, differentiated nonfiction texts to teach language arts standards; DON'T shy away from nonfiction texts.**

To Get Started

Standards before texts. Before we even begin talking about finding nonfiction texts to use to teach the standards, we have to be very familiar with the standards themselves. At this point in your district's adoption of the Common Core State Standards, you may be rolling your eyes, saying to yourself, "How many times can I go over these things?" The answer: Several times, and you will need to keep going over them until you understand what it means for a student to show that they are able to demonstrate the skill, strategy, or idea presented.

In my home state of Ohio, there were many language arts state standards; each one had a single idea, making it relatively easy to create a student target for learning. The Common Core State Standards are more complex; there are fewer of them, but each standard presents multiple ideas and possibly several embedded learning targets that teachers need to tease out. Teasing out the learning targets, or "unpacking the standard" as it is commonly known, is the kind of activity districts have been engaged in as they get ready for full implementation of the CCSS in 2014–2015. Figure 3.1 shows a table containing the Anchor Standards for reading for grades 6–12 with the learning targets embedded within each one for informational text identified for ease of reference.

Figure 3.1   Unpacking the Reading Anchor Standards for Informational Text Skills, Strategies, and Ideas

Reading Anchor Standard	Embedded Skill, Strategy, or Ideas
Read closely to determine what the text says explicitly and to make logical inferences from it; cite specific textual evidence when writing or speaking to support conclusions drawn from the text.	◆ Make inferences ◆ Determine what the text is trying to say ◆ Cite textual evidence when writing or speaking about the text ◆ Draw conclusions from the text
Determine central ideas or themes of a text and analyze their development; summarize the key supporting details and ideas.	◆ Identify central ideas ◆ Identify supporting details ◆ Summarize the text
Analyze how and why individuals, events, and ideas develop and interact over the course of a text.	◆ Trace a process, event, or idea over the course of a text ◆ Analyze why events occur as they do in a text ◆ Describe how elements of a text interact
Interpret words and phrases as they are used in a text, including determining technical, connotative, and figurative meanings, and analyze how specific word choices shape meaning or tone.	◆ Determine the meaning of unknown words and phrases ◆ Analyze how word choice impacts the text

Reading Anchor Standard	Embedded Skill, Strategy, or Ideas
Analyze the structure of texts, including how specific sentences, paragraphs, and larger portions of the text (e.g., a section, chapter, scene, or stanza) relate to each other and the whole.	♦ Identify the text structure ♦ Identify parts of text structure and how they relate to each other
Assess how point of view or purpose shapes the content and style of a text.	♦ Identify author's purpose in writing a text ♦ Identify author's bias in writing about a topic
Integrate and evaluate content presented in diverse formats and media, including visually and quantitatively, as well as in words.	♦ Analyze how charts, maps, and graphs work to enhance a text ♦ Analyze how pictures, captions, and sketches enhance a text
Delineate and evaluate the argument and specific claims in a text, including the validity of the reasoning as well as the relevance and sufficiency of the evidence.	♦ Trace an argument in a text ♦ Evaluate an argument and claims in a text ♦ Evaluate the evidence presented in the argument
Analyze how two or more texts address similar themes or topics in order to build knowledge or to compare the approaches the authors take.	♦ Compare how multiple texts present information on a topic ♦ Read multiple texts on a topic to build knowledge on a topic
Read and comprehend complex literary and informational texts independently and proficiently.	♦ No breakdown necessary!

Choosing an instructional approach. With the standards broken down into individual components, we can now turn our attention to what most language arts teachers like best: the texts. The updated strategies presented below show a different way to use nonfiction in graceful conjunction with traditional fiction texts. However, special attention will be paid to differentiation of texts used with students to meet standard 10: reading texts independently and proficiently. Successful reading opportunities at a student's independent reading level is a sure way to help the learner increase his or her reading level, vocabulary, and writing skills (Routman, 2002).

Instructional Practices to Update

Updated Strategy #1: Twinning Texts to Balance Fiction and Nonfiction in the Language Arts Classroom

Not ready for multiple units based just on nonfiction texts? Twinning texts may be right for you. Born out of watching a group of students struggle with the historical context in *The Book Thief* (Zusak, 2005), the teacher realized that pairing a nonfiction book with a fiction book immediately helped build the background knowledge necessary for students to be able comprehend a book (Baer, 2012). Marzano (2004) identified that background knowledge can account for 33% of the variance in student achievement. It makes sense; if I am reading a historical fiction text or literature that reflects diversity that I do not know much about, I will be relying heavily on my inference skills to fill in the gaps. However, if I had read a book on the topic, I will be more prepared to tackle the knowledge presented in the fiction text (Baer, 2012).

When the need to up the amount of nonfiction reading in our language arts curriculum was presented, some teachers held up articles as proof that they did nonfiction reading. One teacher showed me a unit that centered on the book *Sold* by Patricia McCormick (2006). She introduced the book with an article about child sex slavery. This is the beginning of pairing texts, but it did not do enough to prepare the students for their reading about Nepal, nonwestern cultures and religions, and Indian society (adding more articles to address this is an instructional approach I call "Webbing" that will be discussed in Updated Strategy #2, below). If she paired it with a nonfiction book, like *Little Princes: One Man's Promise to Bring Home the Lost Children of Nepal* (Grennan, 2011), students would be able to immerse themselves in *Sold*, having built their background knowledge through an accessible and more concrete text.

Twinning texts is an easy way to get started on boosting the amount of nonfiction read in the language arts classroom. Beers and Probst (2012) compiled a list of the 25 most commonly used taught novels in grades 4–8. To augment that list, I chose 10 of their books and added 10 of the text exemplars recommended by Appendix B for the Common Core (2011). I then selected nonfiction twin texts to accompany these texts (Figure 3.2). My process for pairing texts is pretty simple:

♦ Know the fiction text you are pairing really well. I often will reread the text and take notes about ideas, terms, and historical perspective that I think my students might struggle with.

♦ Get on the Internet. I wish it was more scientific than this—I found myself looking at the "Customers who bought this title also bought" on Amazon or I scoured book sites like Shelfari and Goodreads for suggested titles.

♦ Check out possibilities. After I narrowed my search, the library and I became fast friends.

♦ READ. You need to read the nonfiction pairing as closely as you read the fiction book. Does it really work? Is it a stretch to make the content connect? Can it be accessed by students who will read at a level of the fiction text? *Is it as good a text as the fiction text?*

Figure 3.2 Twin Texts for 10 of the Most Commonly Taught Novels

Grades 4–8	
Novel	**Twin Text Pairing**
Bud, Not Buddy	Children of the Great Depression
The Cay	Hurricane Dancers: The First Caribbean Pirate Shipwreck
A Christmas Carol	Charles Dickens and the Street Children of London
Hatchet	Into the Wilderness
Maus II: A Survivor's Tale: And Here My Troubles Began	Night
Number the Stars	Darkness Over Denmark: The Danish Resistance and the Rescue of Jews
Roll of Thunder, Hear My Cry	Up Before Daybreak: Cotton and People in America
Tears of a Tiger	The 6 Most Important Decisions You'll Ever Make: A Guide for Teens
To Kill a Mockingbird	They Called Themselves the KKK: The Birth of an American Terrorist Group
The Watsons Go to Birmingham—1963	We've Got a Job: The 1963 Birmingham Children's March

Grades 9–12	
Novel	**Twin Text Pairing**
The Adventures of Tom Sawyer	The Trouble Begins at 8: A Life of Mark Twain in the Wild, Wild West
The Adventures of Huckleberry Finn	See above
The Great Gatsby	Bootleg: Murder, Moonshine, and the Lawless Years of Prohibition
Animal Farm	Tsar: The Lost World of Nicholas and Alexandra
The Joy Luck Club	Red Scarf Girl
The Book Thief	Hitler Youth: Growing Up in Hitler's Shadow
Lord of the Flies	Island of the Lost: Shipwrecked at the Edge of the world
The Crucible	Witches! The Absolutely True Tale of Disaster in Salem
The Grapes of Wrath	Up Close: John Steinbeck
Romeo and Juliet	Shakespeare: His Work and World

Differentiation. I am hoping that teachers don't view the twin texts idea as a pass to go back to "one book, one class!" I really see twin texts as an opportunity to have students participate in literature circles for fiction texts (Daniels, 2002) and "Textmasters" for nonfiction texts (Wilfong, 2009). The teacher will book talk the texts to be read, students will rank which books they wish to read, and the teacher can match readers up by preference and reading level. Groups will then work their way through both a fiction and nonfiction text, using the role sheets for both strategies to guide close reading, discussion, and comprehension. If literature circles are not your thing, then paired texts can be used to facilitate small group reading with older students—guided reading with equal attention to fiction and nonfiction.

Updated Strategy #2: Webbing an Anchor Text to Provide
Nonfiction Text Support

The last strategy to update your instructional process in choosing and using nonfiction—Webbing—was briefly touched upon in the previous section. Webbing occurs when teachers take a central, fiction text and then surround it with a variety of texts to facilitate comprehension of topics presented in the novel. This strategy is great for teachers not yet ready to commit to teaching full, nonfiction books but who see the value in implementing a variety of articles to support student comprehension. This strategy can also be a great way to really pair standards with nonfiction text: the teacher identifies a topic that students need more background information on in a fiction text (like sharecropping in *Roll of Thunder, Hear My Cry*) and then searches out a brief article. The structure of the article can lend itself to different teaching strategies that hit specific standards, perfect for minilessons. Figure 3.3 shows a sample web, with a central text in the middle and identified topics that students might need support with.

Figure 3.3 Webbing for *Jasper Jones*

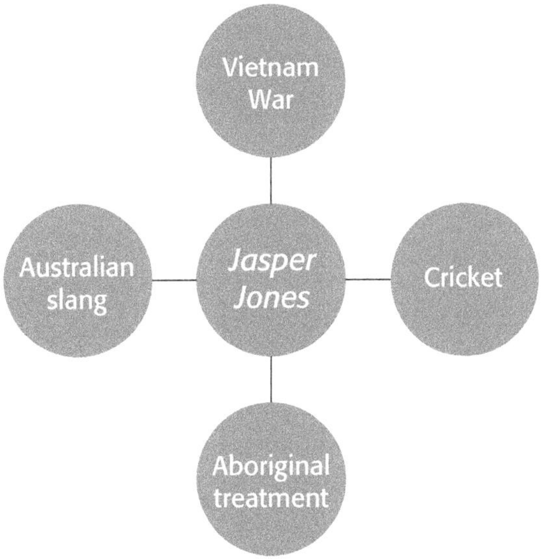

After identifying these topics for study, it is up to the teacher to find appropriate nonfiction articles to use in instruction. I have two go-to resources for nonfiction articles: Middle Search Plus and Mas Ultra, both located on EbscoHost. These search engines (widely available in libraries across the nation) allow you to search by topic, Lexile, even text type (primary source document, periodical, etc.).

Differentiation. Most teachers, when using this kind of system, are thinking of whole class instruction—read the novel together, with the nonfiction articles thrown in for support as needed. I like to think of this system as being just as adaptable to differentiation. The whole class reads the central novel with support from the teacher. The nonfiction articles are leveled and students are assigned different articles depending on their reading challenges and strengths. I have also seen teachers give groups of students a particular topic to research and present to the class in conjunction with reading the central novel, making each group an expert on an idea in the text.

Flipping this idea, one school district decided to go with a Webbing approach but instead of one central novel, they chose a theme with a list of several novels from which students could choose (based on interest and reading level) (Morgan et al., 2013). The nonfiction articles were used in small groups by standard, based on a pretest, allowing for fluid group membership and support for the more difficult nonfiction articles as needed.

Common Core Connection

The strategies presented above fit well with a variety of standards in the Common Core State Standards for English Language Arts. However, one main standard is addressed by the simple idea of adding more informational text to the language arts curriculum.

Figure 3.4 Common Core State Standards Addressed in this Chapter

Grade Level	4–10
Standard Addressed	**Reading Standards for Informational Text**
	By the end of the year, read and comprehend informational texts.

Conclusion

Incorporating more nonfiction text into the language arts curriculum takes careful planning and time to read, read, read. It's time to take some action:

1. Which instructional update appeals to you most? Why?

   _____

   _____

   _____

   _____

2. If you are planning on Twinning Texts or Webbing, use one of the planning graphic organizers to help you organize your ideas:

Works Cited

Baer, A. (2012). Pairing books for learning: The union of informational and fiction. *The History Teacher, 45*, 283–395.

Beers, K., & Probst, R. E. (2012). *Notice and note: Strategies for close reading*. Portsmouth, NH; Heinemann.

Daniels, H. (2002). *Literature circles: Voice and choice in book clubs and reading groups*. New York: Stenhouse.

Grennan, C. (2011). *Little princes: One man's promise to bring home the lost children of Nepal*. New York: William Morrow.

Marzano, R. J. (2004). *Building background knowledge for academic achievement: Research on what works in schools*. Alexandria, VA: ASCD.

McCormick, P. (2006). *Sold*. New York: Hyperion.

Morgan, D., Williams, J., Clark, B., Hatteberg, S., Hauptman, G., Kozel, C., & Paris, J. (2013). Guiding readers in middle grades. *Middle School Journal, 44*, 16–24.

National Governors Association for Best Practices, Council of Chief State School Officers. (2011). Appendix B (English language arts). Washington, DC: Author

Porter, A., McMaken, J., Hwang, J., & Yang, R. (2011). Common Core standards: The new U.S. intended curriculum. *Educational Researcher, 40*, 103–116.

Routman, R. (2002). *Reading essentials: The specifics you need to teach reading well*. Portsmouth, NH: Heinemann.

Wilfong, L. G. (2009). Textmasters: Bringing literature circles to textbook reading across the curriculum. *Journal of Adolescent and Adult Literacy, 53*, 164–171.

Zusak, M. (2005). *The book thief*. Boston: Knopf.

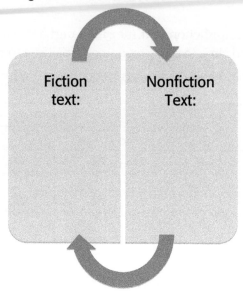

Fiction text:

Nonfiction Text:

Copyright 2014 Taylor & Francis. All rights reserved. www.routledge.com

Template 3.2 Webbing

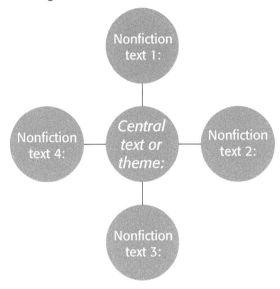

Copyright 2014 Taylor & Francis. All rights reserved. www.routledge.com

Chapter 4

Purposefully Select and Study Vocabulary Words to Support Nonfiction Reading

The teachers flipped through "Letter from Birmingham Jail," a nonfiction text highlighted in many Common Core documents as an exemplar for use with the informational text reading standards. "I don't even know where to begin!" exclaimed one teacher, tossing the paper on the table in front of her in frustration. "This is powerful stuff but it seems so hard for high school students!" Her tablemate kept skimming, pen in hand: "I start with the words that I think will be hard for them to understand," she stated. "I'm up to twenty so far and I am on the third page. That will get my students started on understanding what this text is about."

Why Is This Item on the List So Important?

It is common for language arts teachers to approach the teaching of a text through its vocabulary; after all, when we use our teacher guides and novel packs to plan instruction, we are often gifted with a list of vocabulary words to accompany each short story or chapter. But when we begin to do more than rely on premade materials to develop curricular units, it is up to us to strategically select words that challenge and support our students in their comprehension of a text. And, as we learned in the previous chapter, finding and using quality nonfiction often means going outside traditional sources!

Vocabulary does comprise a large part of comprehension. In 1977, Cunningham and Stanovich found that vocabulary assessed in first grade predicted 30% of reading variance in 11th grade. We need to honor this relationship by choosing words carefully and implementing great strategies to help students take ownership of new and vital words that can be transferred into future reading and writing.

> Do this—not that principle #4: DO purposefully select and study vocabulary words to support nonfiction reading. DON'T rely on textbooks to dictate which words to teach and how to teach them.

To Get Started

Full disclosure: I have written an entire book devoted to the selection, study, and assessment of vocabulary across the content areas ☺. I am passionate about the topic and have enjoyed working with teachers as they learn how to discard traditional vocabulary strategies and update their practice with new ones. I always like to start this discussion with some basic, shocking facts:

1. In order for students to move up a grade level in their reading, they need to learn between 3,000 and 5,000 words a year. An expert teacher, through direct instruction, can only teach about 350 words a year (Baumann, Edwards, Boland, Olejnik, & Kame'enui, 2003).

2. Students can only cognitively handle 8–10 new vocabulary words a week; most teachers use lists of 20 or more words a week, depending on the topic being studied (Scott, Jamieson-Noel, & Asselin, 2003; Wilfong, 2012).

3. Textbook publishers do not generally have a scientific way of selecting words for study to accompany text; the focus is on multisyllabic words or words that are repeated in later chapters (Nagy, 2008).

In order to think about how to update language arts teachers' instructional practices, we will focus on three areas: selection of vocabulary for instructional focus, strategies to promote independence in attacking unknown words, and strategies to use during word study time.

Instructional Practices to Update

Updated Strategy #1: Selecting Words for Instructional Focus

In our limited instructional time, being picky about what words we choose for vocabulary instruction is very important! I have found that many teachers feel somewhat freed when we talk about discarding the long lists publishers give them in favor of creating shorter, more selective lists to use in conjunction with texts. However, to do this, some advance work is needed in order to know that we are truly selecting the right words for study.

Tiering words to help with selection of vocabulary words to study is a relatively painless but interesting process. Developed by Beck, McKeown, and Kucan (2002), tiering asks teachers to take a list of words (could be a publisher-manufactured list or a teacher-generated list) and to think about the context in which the text presents it. They then place the words into the appropriate tiers. The three tiers are as follows:

Tier 1—General/Conversational words
Commonplace; learned from interactions with texts and people
Tier 2—Polysemic (multiple meaning)
Changes meaning depending on context
Tier 3—Content-specific/Technical
Specific to the discipline being studied

Once your list is placed into tiers, you have an idea of which words to focus on. Beck et al. (2002) advocate for the majority of your direct instruction time to focus on Tier 2 words. Words that are polysemic, or have multiple meanings, are power words in the English language; when we understand the various meanings that a polysemic word has, we have access to its multiple uses in multiple contexts (Wilfong, 2012). This may seem counterintuitive; many teachers immediately jump to Tier 3 words as the words of focus. While these words are still important, they are not the words that should be used in strategies with students. Fisher and Frey (2008) feel that these words can be taught quickly to students through frontloading and do not merit an abundance of time; show a student what Tier 3 words mean, maybe through a quick PowerPoint slide show, with each slide containing the word and a picture to help illustrate the meaning, and then move on with life. Figure 4.1 presents a list of vocabulary words for a portion of "Letter from Birmingham Jail" and then shows how the words could be tiered to select which words to focus on for instruction for a ninth grade class.

Figure 4.1   Tiered Vocabulary Words for "Letter from Birmingham Jail"

Tier 1—General
Humiliate creatively action demonstration urge consistently voluntarily

Tier 2—Polysemic
Precipitate engage register posture foster spring

Tier 3—Content-Specific
Segregate tension categorize scintillate structured commend relegate community integrate sanctimonious oppress existential inevitability engulf reiterate advocate

---

By tiering the words, we were able to cut a list of 29 down to six for deep study. It is usually at this point that someone points out the long list that remains in Tier 3. That is why including strategies in your classroom for students to use to attack words independently is so important—Updated Strategy #2!

Updated Strategy #2: Teaching Greek and Latin Roots and Affixes to Promote Independence in Word Attack Skills

Because simply memorizing definitions of vocabulary words does little to promote word recognition, students need strategies to assist them in attacking unknown words used in a text. The use of context clues is one type of word attack skill that teachers employ to help students figure out the meaning of a variety of words—prompting students to use the local sentence, and sentences preceding and following, and to look for signal punctuation or words that help clue the reader into the fact that the author is helping to define the word for them (Beers, 2002; Wilfong 2012).

Beyond context clues is the use of explicit instruction in a variety of Greek and Latin roots and affixes to help students breakdown multisyllabic words. The Common Core State Standards (2011), in all their wisdom, include a standard about the use of Greek and Latin roots and affixes to figure out unknown words as early as first grade. A Greek and Latin word study routine, as a regular part of any language arts classroom, is an excellent way to support student vocabulary growth. Consider the following:

♦ Nearly two out of every three multisyllabic words in the English language contain a Greek or Latin root or affix (Bromley, 2007).

♦ One Greek or Latin root or affix can give students access to an average of 20 or more English words (Rasinski, Padak, Newton, & Newton, 2010).

The following word study routine was originally developed by Casey Ober-hauser, a seventh grade teacher in Maple Heights City Schools in Northeast Ohio, to assist her students in feeling confident to breakdown unknown words (Wilfong, Oberhauser, & Smedley, 2013):

> **Monday:** Introduce/pre-assess the root or affix of the week through a word sort. Give students an envelope containing slips of paper with a variety of words using the root/affix of the week in different ways. Ask students to sort the slips in a way that makes sense to them. Words sorts allow teachers to quickly see what kind of knowledge a student already has about a word part—do students recognize that the word stems can occur in different parts of the word (beginning, middle, or end)? Do students sort by meaning? The rationale of *how* the word sort was organized gives the teacher insight into student thinking about new words (Fisher, Brozo, Frey, & Ivey, 2011; Fisher & Frey, 2011; Wilfong, 2012; Wilfong et al., 2013). After the word sort, the teacher can do a thorough introduction of the word part of the week: What it is and what it means. An example of a set of word sort slips is shown in Figure 4.2.

Figure 4.2 A Sample Set of Word Sort Cards Using the Root *Port* (from the Latin meaning carry)

IMPORTANT	EXPORT	IMPORT
REPORT	DEPORTATION	RAPPORT
PORTLY	PORTAGE	INSUPPORTABLE

> **Tuesday:** Invite students deeper into the study of the word part of the week; ask them to brainstorm a variety of words that contain the root or affix, using the word tree template. This template, presented in sample form in Figure 4.3, below, and as template at the end of the chapter, can be distributed to students to use individually or in groups, or enlarged and posted in the classroom to complete as a whole class activity. Over the course of the semester, students can post additional words that contain the word part on the class poster or on their individual word trees to reinforce the meaning of this particular word part.

Figure 4.3 Sample Word Tree Template, Using the Latin Root *Port*

Wednesday: Assist students in dissecting words, using the meaning of the root. A Concept Map is a simple a way to help students think about the meaning of a word through its synonyms, antonyms, and nonlinguistic representation of text (drawing) (Beers, 2002; Wilfong, 2012). Distribute the Concept Map template to students (see a sample in Figure 4.4 and in Template 4.2 at the end of the chapter). Have students select one word from the word tree and complete a Concept Map. Model one example with students, showing how you use the meaning of the root to help you write a short definition of the word.

Figure 4.4 Sample Concept Map Using the Latin Root *Port*

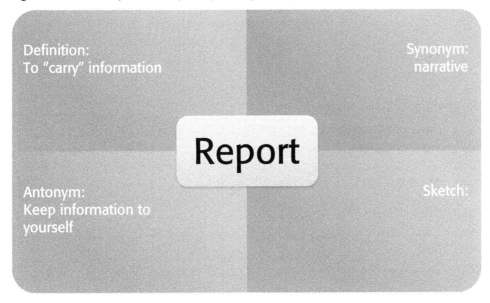

Thursday: Game day! So many fun vocabulary word games are out there but one of Casey's seventh graders favorite games was Wordo. In this take on Bingo, the teacher distributes a Wordo card filled out with words containing the word part of the week (use a Bingo card generator like www.teachnology. com/web_tools/materials/bingo/ to create Wordo cards with the words distributed in different ways). Announce what type of game you will play ("X," "Four Corners," "Diagonal Line," etc.). Then, call out the definitions of the words, stressing the use of the word part. When a student is able to create the shape of the game being played, they call out "Wordo!" This is a fun way to review the use of the word part.

Friday: Time to check and see if a student is able to use the word correctly in context. Being able to write with the words is considered the ultimate application of new word knowledge. To this end, create a prompt that will allow students to write a paragraph using the words appropriately. Figure 4.5 contains a sample prompt, student response, and rubric that were used to check for understanding and application of the word part of the week.

Figure 4.5   Sample Assessment for the Word Part *Port*

Prompt: You would like to start a company that ships goods overseas and brings goods from other countries to the United States. Write a one paragraph proposal about what this company intends to do, using as many words containing the word part *port*.

Student response:

Our company, Krug Importing and Exporting, proposes to create relations with a variety of overseas companies, to import and export goods to the United States. By starting this company, we will support good relations between the United States and other countries. We will report our earnings each quarter.

Rubric:

	3	2	1
Use of target word part	Student is able to use the word part of the week correctly at least four times.	Students is able to use the word part of the week correctly at least two times.	Student is able to use the word part of the week correctly one time.

The beauty of this word study routine is the brevity of each of the strategies. Each daily activity takes between 5 and 15 minutes to implement (longer in the beginning, as you model and support students in learning the routine). The entire language arts department at Casey's school adopted this word study routine, sequencing a variety of Greek and Latin root words for study.

Updated Strategy #3: Contrasting Academic Language with Vocabulary Presented in a Text

The last key update for language arts teachers focusing on nonfiction text to consider is the contrast between academic language and the vocabulary presented in a text. This idea is a departure from how a content area teacher uses a piece of text. The content area teacher uses a piece of text to teach specific content, i.e., a biology teacher using an article about Colony Collapse Disorder to discuss the effects of pesticides on the bee population. A language arts teacher uses a nonfiction text to teach a specific skill, i.e., summarize, infer, compare and contrast. Therefore, our approach to the vocabulary to focus on must differ from that of our content area colleagues, too.

A definition of academic language will augment this discussion. It has been described as the "language of schooling" (Zwiers, 2007) but more specifically, it is the vocabulary critical to understanding the concepts of the content taught in school (Marzano & Pickering, 2005). The vocabulary of reading and writing, the domains of language arts teacher, are not necessarily the words students encounter in texts; rather, they are the words of the skills and concepts we teach students to be excellent readers and writers, themselves!

In Strategy #1, above, we talked about tiering the vocabulary to find "power" words to focus on, words with multiple meanings that will go beyond simply learning a word to comprehend the text at hand. We can supplement these words by thinking about our intention of using this text in our classroom, which stems from the standard or standards we are focusing on in conjunction with this text. So, let's start with the standards.

Let's say that I am a sixth grade teacher and my curriculum map shows that our next Reading Informational Text standard to emphasize in instruction is RI 6.2: *Determine a central idea of a text and how it is conveyed through particular details; provide a summary of the text distinct from personal opinions or judgments.* Within the standard itself lies the academic language that students need to know to be successful: *central idea, details,* and *summary* free of bias. These words will help a student know what to accomplish, essentially, the language of the discipline, rather than simply memorizing words that will help them comprehend a text. Table 4.1 shows a breakdown of the academic language of the Reading Informational Text standards at the sixth grade level.

Table 4.1 Breakdown of the Academic Language Presented in the Reading Informational Text Standards at Sixth Grade

Standard	Academic Language
RI 6.1 Cite textual evidence to support analysis of what the text says explicitly as well as inferences drawn from the text.	♦ Cite ♦ Textual evidence ♦ Inference
RI 6.2 Determine a central idea of a text and how it is conveyed through particular details; provide a summary of the text distinct from personal opinions or judgments.	♦ Central idea ♦ Details ♦ Summary
RI 6.3 Analyze in detail how a key individual, event, or idea is introduced, illustrated, and elaborated in a text (e.g., through examples or anecdotes).	♦ Introduce ♦ Illustrate ♦ Elaborate ♦ Anecdotes

Standard	Academic Language
RI 6.4 Determine the meaning of words and phrases as they are used in a text, including figurative, connotative, and technical meanings.	♦ Figurative meaning ♦ Connotative meaning ♦ Technical meaning
RI 6.5 Analyze how a particular sentence, paragraph, chapter, or section fits into the overall structure of a text and contributes to the development of the ideas.	♦ Sentence, paragraph, chapter, section ♦ Structure of a text ♦ Analyze
RI 6.6 Determine an author's point of view or purpose in a text and explain how it is conveyed in the text.	♦ Author's point of view ♦ Convey
RI 6.7 Integrate information presented in different media or formats (e.g., visually, quantitatively) as well as in words to develop a coherent understanding of a topic or issue.	♦ Integrate ♦ Media ♦ Coherent understanding
RI 6.8 Trace and evaluate the argument and specific claims in a text, distinguishing claims that are supported by reasons and evidence from claims that are not.	♦ Trace ♦ Evaluate ♦ Argument ♦ Specific claims ♦ Distinguish
RI 6.9 Compare and contrast one author's presentation of events with that of another (e.g., a memoir written by and a biography on the same person).	♦ Compare ♦ Contrast ♦ Presentation of events
RI 6.10 By the end of the year, read and comprehend literary nonfiction in the grades 6–8 text complexity band proficiently, with scaffolding as needed at the high end of the range.	♦ Comprehend ♦ Literary nonfiction

Therefore, as we move forward in implementing the use of more nonfiction texts in our classroom, we must consider the academic language that students need to be able to read and write in response to these texts, as well as the words in the texts, themselves, that will help them comprehend what they read.

Common Core Connection

The strategies presented above fit well with a variety of standards in the Common Core State Standards for English Language Arts (see Figure 4.6).

Figure 4.6 Common Core State Standards Addressed in this Chapter

Grade Level	4	5	6
Standard Addressed	**Reading Standards for Informational Text** Determine the meaning of general academic and domain-specific words or phrases in a text relevant to a *Grade 4 topic or subject area.* **Language** Use common, grade appropriate Greek and Latin affixes as clues to the meaning of a word. Demonstrate understanding of words by relating them to their opposites (antonyms) and to words with similar but not identical meanings (synonyms).	**Reading Standards for Informational Text** Determine the meaning of general academic and domain-specific words or phrases in a text relevant to a *Grade 5 topic or subject area.* **Language** Use common, grade appropriate Greek and Latin affixes as clues to the meaning of a word. Use the relationship between particular words to better understand each of the words.	**Reading Standards for Informational Text** Determine the meaning of words and phrases as they are used in a text, including figurative, connotative, and technical meanings. **Language** Use common, grade-appropriate Greek or Latin affixes and roots as clues to the meaning of a word (e.g., *audience, auditory, audible*).

Grade Level	7	8	9–10
Standard Addressed	**Reading Standards for Informational Text** Determine the meaning of words and phrases as they are used in a text, including figurative, connotative, and technical meanings; analyze the impact of a specific word choice on meaning and tone. **Language** Use common, grade-appropriate Greek or Latin affixes and roots as clues to the meaning of a word (e.g., *belligerent, bellicose, rebel*).	**Reading Standards for Informational Text** Determine the meaning of words and phrases as they are used in a text, including figurative, connotative, and technical meanings; analyze the impact of specific word choices on meaning and tone, including analogies or allusions to other texts. **Language** Use common, grade-appropriate Greek or Latin affixes and roots as clues to the meaning of a word (e.g., *precede, recede, secede*).	**Reading Standards for Informational Text** Determine the meaning of words and phrases as they are used in a text, including figurative, connotative, and technical meanings; analyze the cumulative impact of specific word choices on meaning and tone (e.g., how the language of a court opinion differs from that of a newspaper). **Language** Identify and correctly use patterns of word changes that indicate different meanings or parts of speech (e.g., *analyze, analysis, analytical; advocate, advocacy*).

Conclusion

It is obvious that intentional selection and instruction of vocabulary in conjunction with nonfiction texts is an important element in language instruction. It is time to take some action . . .

1. Select a Reading Informational Text standard to focus on for an upcoming instructional unit. Write out the standard below:

_____

_____

_____

_____

2. What is the academic language that needs attention when working with students on learning this standard? Record the academic language in the box below:

```
┌─────────────────────────────────────────────┐
│                                             │
│                                             │
│                                             │
│                                             │
└─────────────────────────────────────────────┘
```

3. Now, select a text to use to help students work through this standard. Write the title of the text here:

_____

4. Look through the text for words that will aid in comprehension of the material. List the words here:

_____

_____

_____

_____

5. Tier the words you selected to help you figure out which text-based words to focus on in instruction.

    Tier 1:

    Tier 2:

    Tier 3:

6. Challenge: Do any of your words in Tier 2 or 3 have a Greek or Latin root or affix? If so, create a word sort with a variety of words using that word part in the template below:

Works Cited

Baumann, J., Edwards, E., Boland, E., Olejnik, S., & Kame'enui, E. (2003). Vocabulary tricks: Effects of instruction in morphology and context on fifth-grade students' ability to derive and infer word meanings. *American Educational Research Journal, 40,* 447–494.

Beck, I. L., McKeown, M. G., & Kucan, L. (2002). *Bringing words to life: Robust vocabulary instruction.* New York: Guilford.

Beers, K. (2002). *When kids can't read—what teachers can do: A guide for teachers 6–12.* Portsmouth, NH: Heinemann.

Bromley, K. (2007). Nine things every teacher should know about vocabulary instruction. *Journal of Adolescent and Adult Literacy, 50,* 528–537.

Cunningham, A., & Stanovich, K. (1977). Early reading acquisition and its relation to reading experience and ability 10 years later. *Developmental Psychology, 33,* 934–945.

Fisher, D., Brozo, W., Frey, N., & Ivey, G. (2011). *50 instructional routines to develop content literacy.* Boston: Pearson.

Fisher, D., & Frey, N. (2008). *Word wise and content rich, grades 7–12.* Portsmouth, NH: Heinemann.

Fisher, D., & Frey, N. (2011). *Improving adolescent literacy: Content area strategies at work* (3rd ed.). Boston: Allyn & Bacon.

Marzano, R., & Pickering, D. (2005). *Building academic vocabulary: Teacher's manual.* Alexandria, VA: ASCD.

Nagy, W. (2008, October). *Choosing words to teach: Beyond Tier Two.* Paper presented at the meeting of International Reading Association, West Regional Conference, Seattle, OR.

National Governors Association for Best Practices, Council of Chief State School Officers. (2011). Common core state standards (English language arts). Washington, DC: Author.

Rasinski, T., Padak, N., Newton, J., & Newton, E. (2010). The Latin-Greek connection: Building vocabulary through morphological study. *The Reading Teacher, 65,* 133–141.

Scott, J. A., Jamieson-Noel, D., & Asselin, M. (2003). Vocabulary instruction throughout the day in 23 Canadian upper-elementary classrooms. *Elementary School Journal, 103,* 269–268.

Wilfong, L. G. (2012). *Do this, not that! An eye on updating your vocabulary practices, grades 4–9.* New York: Routledge.

Wilfong, L. G., Oberhauser, C., & Smedley, R. (2013). Words, words, words! Making word study a priority in middle school across content areas. *In Perspective, 9,* 12–14.

Zwiers, J. (2007). Teacher practices and perspectives for developing academic language. *International Journal of Applied Linguistics, 17,* 93–116.

Template 4.1 Word Tree Template

Copyright 2014 Taylor & Francis. All rights reserved. www.routledge.com

Template 4.2 Concept Map Template

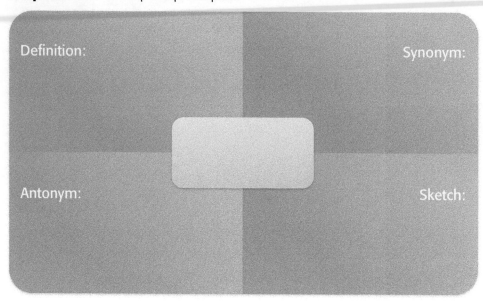

Definition:

Synonym:

Antonym:

Sketch:

Copyright 2014 Taylor & Francis. All rights reserved. www.routledge.com

Work with Content Area Colleagues to Select Nonfiction Topics that Cross the Curriculum

After reading an excerpt from Johnny Tremain (Forbes, 1943) with the fifth graders, we discussed the different historical figures present. "Ben Franklin!" "John Adams!" students shouted out. I explained that we would be writing "I Am" poems from the point of view of one of the fictional characters or one of the historical figures from the text. Keisha waited patiently with her hand up: "Mrs. W., this is language arts class. We are talking about the Revolutionary War in Social Studies class." I responded that I had talked to Mr. Harper about what he was teaching and picked this book to go along with what they were studying in his class. "Is that okay?" I asked her, smiling. She responded, "It just feels weird. I didn't know you talked to each other."

Why Is This Item on the List So Important?

Keisha quickly summed up the issue at hand—just as our students don't often believe that we don't live at the school, they also don't believe that it is possible for teachers of different content areas to interact. And I don't blame her! Integrating the curriculum was huge in the 1990s, especially in the middle school arena, as the idea of teaming was first brought up and teachers worked together to create curricula that crossed all content areas to support student learning (Gehrke, 1998), but the movement waned as teachers were faced with more mandates that needed to be carried out in their individual classrooms. However, these cross-curricular conversations may be just the thing to help bring appropriate nonfiction texts into the language arts classroom.

If you are a social studies or science teacher reading this, you might be saying, "It's about time!" For over a decade now, content area literacy has been stressed in these classrooms (Benjamin, 2007; Vacca, Vacca, & Mraz, 2013). Summarizing, close reading, and vocabulary study were no longer isolated skills in the reading and writing classroom; content area teachers were "helping" language arts teachers out by using them to teach their own content.

It is time to pay it forward—as language arts teachers, we are able to teach the skills and strategies necessary for students to master informational text through complex and rigorous readings on a variety of subjects. Why not support student learning across disciplines by finding texts that emphasize content being taught in their science, social studies, math, or unified arts classrooms?

> *Do this—not that principle #5: DO work with content area colleagues to select nonfiction topics that cross the curriculum; DON'T work in isolation on nonfiction topics.*

To Get Started

Wait! Breathe! Before you start getting all huffy, thinking that I am asking you to teach social studies or science *content,* hear me out! One of the first moments of panic I experienced with teachers was when I was examining the high school English/language arts informational text reading standards, which reference U.S. foundational texts as a document for supporting student analytic reading (CCSS, 2011). We opened up the Bill of Rights, a document that most of us have not cracked since U.S. History our freshmen year in college. The room was silent as we scanned the lines. One teacher closed her book and looked defiantly around the room. "I am an *English* teacher, not a Social Studies teacher! I don't know how to teach this stuff!" Other teachers looked up from their reading with true panic in their eyes. Another responded, "Is that what they want? For us to teach Social Studies?"

This is a paradigm shift for language arts teachers. We are not being asked to teach the content of the Bill of Rights (or other foundational U.S. documents); rather, we are being asked to help students have the ability to analyze the content for meaning, structure, and author craft. This kind of reading screams for cross-curricular support; a conversation between the social studies teacher and language arts teacher that might go something like this:

> Language Arts teacher: "Hey (fill in the name of your Social Studies teacher). In your U.S. History class, when do you cover the Bill of Rights?"
>
> Social Studies teacher: "Well, (fill in your name), I will be teaching it in (month). Why?"
>
> Language Arts teacher: "Okay. I would like to use the text in my room for students to read and analyze. Perhaps you can introduce it first in your room and then we will analyze it my room."
>
> Social Studies teacher: "Wow, that would be great."

In the real world, these conversations can be hard to have, which is why district curriculum maps or pacing guides can help clue the language arts teacher in to when different topics are being studied across disciplines.

Instructional Practices to Update

Updated Strategy #1: Letting Your Content Area Colleagues' Topics Guide Your Unit Creation

I am going to make a loaded statement: The language arts, defined as reading, writing, speaking, and listening, are content area-less. We are not a traditional content area in that we have a clearly defined package of knowledge that students will leave our classroom with (e.g., biology, where students leave with knowledge of cells, DNA, genetic variation, etc.). Instead, we have something bigger: the goal to help every student leave our classroom a better reader, writer, speaker, and listener in order to help them in their mastery of the more traditional content areas.

I made that statement to a middle school group of language arts teachers who first looked at me with astonishment and then resignation. By agreeing to this statement, they opened themselves up to the idea of letting other content area topics guide their text selection for use in their instruction.

Informational text-based units. The eighth grade language arts team decided to have a nonfiction focus each month, spotlighting a topic from their content area colleagues. They rotated the spotlight between science, social studies, math, and physical education, the latter being the most popular selection with the students. As an additional challenge, they tried to pair a fiction text with the nonfiction focus of the month, a twist on the twinning text strategy from Chapter 3; most teachers twin texts with the fiction text as the primary text. Table 5.1 shows the first four months of fiction and nonfiction reading in those eighth grade classrooms.

Table 5.1 Cross-curricular Fiction and Nonfiction Reading in Eighth Grade

Month	Content area spotlight	Nonfiction focus (2–3 short articles or book excerpts)	Fiction anchor text
September	Science	Theory of Evolution	*The Evolution of Calpurnia Tate* (Kelly, 2011)
October	Social Studies	Revolutionary War	*Chains* (Anderson, 2010)
November	Math	Pythagoras Theorem	*The Curious Incident of the Dog in the Night-time* (Haddon, 2003)
December	Physical Education	Basketball	*Boy 21* (Quick, 2012)

After selecting and studying the texts in depth, the team worked together to match each unit with a set of standards.

Nonfiction Fridays. The seventh grade language arts team at this school was not ready for such implementation and decided instead to borrow an idea from Kelly Gallagher's *Readicide* (2009), called Article of the Week. Initially developed to help students have a better grasp on current events, it has evolved into a national movement of language arts teachers using informational text in engaging ways in the classroom. The seventh grade team capitalized on this idea by deciding to focus on content area topics for an article of the week, rather than current events. They felt that this freed them to continue working on their more traditional, fiction-based curriculum map while beginning to incorporate the nonfiction text that their students needed. They shortened their fiction teaching of reading and writing to a Monday through Thursday schedule and then designated Fridays to be "Nonfiction Fridays." They also used their colleagues' curriculum maps, but quarterly; first and third quarter emphasized topics from science and second and fourth quarter emphasized topics from social studies. The team consisted of eight teachers. They split up the nine-week quarter, designating a week for each teacher to consult the appropriate curriculum map, find an article or two that correlated with the topic being taught in the content area class, and distribute it to the rest of the language arts colleagues (week nine in the quarter was left open to allow teachers an extra day for catch up, if needed). An electronic storage website was used to post each article, along with teaching ideas.

Updated Strategy #2: Using a Framework to Support Collaboration with Content Area Colleagues

The idea for a framework to support collaboration between language arts and content area colleagues came about in a recent professional development session I held with social studies and science teachers who received their initial introduction to the Literacy Standards for History/Social Studies, Science and Other Technical Subjects (CCSS, 2011). They brought up their language arts colleagues' need to find more nonfiction for their own classrooms. "What if," a science teacher proposed, "we came up with a model that we could use that showed the central topic, the introductory reading and teaching on the topic the science or social studies teacher would do, and then the supportive reading on the topic the language arts teachers could do?" This idea resonated with the other science and social studies teachers, but how would it come across to language arts teachers?

It turns out, that this framework became a great place to begin cross-content area collaborations. The science teacher who proposed the idea above showed the framework in Figure 5.1, below, to his language arts teammate.

Figure 5.1   A Framework for Supporting Cross-content Area Reading

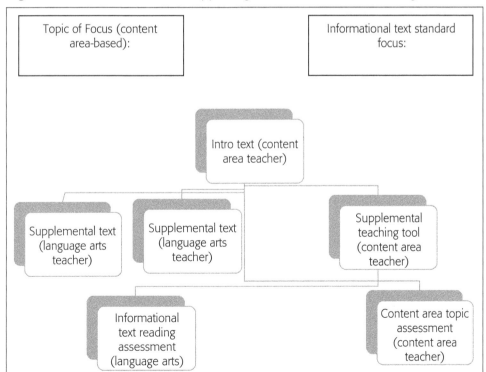

The division of labor helped show a timeline for introduction of the topic and its teaching tools, as well as giving a clear picture of who would be assessing what, and showing that the language arts teacher would focus on the informational text standards and the content area teacher will assess the actual content. Figure 5.2 shows a filled out framework, used by the teachers referenced above to create a language arts/science unit.

Figure 5.2   A Completed Framework for Supporting Cross-content Area Reading

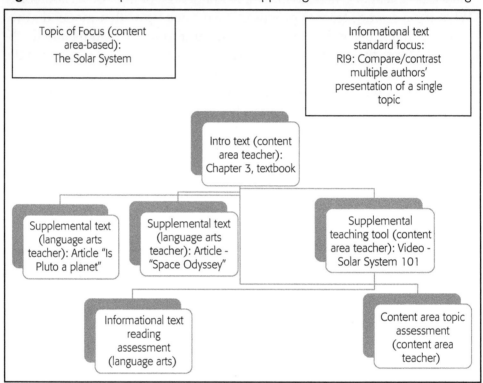

The language arts teacher was enthusiastic about the framework. "It was an easy way for me to think about supporting science topics in my classroom and providing some great cross-curricular conversations in the classroom. I learned alongside my students about the solar system but was able to support them in their reading of these difficult, nonfiction texts on a topic they were actually interested in." She was especially pleased how this framework supported the teaching of Reading Informational Text #9: Comparing/contrasting how multiple authors present information on the same topic. "I wasn't sure how I would teach this standard previously," she stated. "But relying on my science counterpart to introduce the topic through a different text took the burden off of me trying to do all the work by teaching all the texts!"

Common Core Connection

The strategies presented above fit well with a variety of standards in the Common Core State Standards for English Language Arts (see Figure 5.3).

Figure 5.3 Common Core State Standards Addressed in this Chapter

Grade Level	4	5	6
Standard Addressed	**Reading Standards for Informational Text** Explain events, procedures, ideas, or concepts in a historical, scientific, or technical text, including what happened and why, based on specific information in the text. Integrate information from two texts on the same topic in order to write or speak about the subject knowledgeably. By the end of year, read and comprehend informational texts, including history/social studies, science, and technical texts, in the grades 4–5 text complexity band proficiently, with scaffolding as needed at the high end of the range.	**Reading Standards for Informational Text** Explain the relationships or interactions between two or more individuals, events, ideas, or concepts in a historical, scientific, or technical text based on specific information in the text. Analyze multiple accounts of the same event or topic, noting important similarities and differences in the point of view they represent. Draw on information from multiple print or digital sources, demonstrating the ability to locate an answer to a question quickly or to solve a problem efficiently. Integrate information from several texts on the same topic in order to write or speak about the subject knowledgeably. By the end of year, read and comprehend informational texts, including history/social studies, science, and technical texts, in the grades 4–5 text complexity band proficiently, with scaffolding as needed at the high end of the range.	**Reading Standards for Informational Text** Integrate information presented in different media or formats (e.g., visually, quantitatively) as well as in words to develop a coherent understanding of a topic or issue. Compare and contrast one author's presentation of events with that of another (e.g., a memoir written by and a biography on the same person). By the end of the year, read and comprehend literary nonfiction in the grades 6–8 text complexity band proficiently, with scaffolding as needed at the high end of the range.

Grade Level	7	8	9–10
Standard Addressed	**Reading Standards for Informational Text** Compare and contrast a text to an audio, video, or multimedia version of the text, analyzing each medium's portrayal of the subject (e.g., how the delivery of a speech affects the impact of the words). Analyze how two or more authors writing about the same topic shape their presentations of key information by emphasizing different evidence or advancing different interpretations of facts. By the end of the year, read and comprehend literary nonfiction in the grades 6–8 text complexity band proficiently, with scaffolding as needed at the high end of the range.	**Reading Standards for Informational Text** Evaluate the advantages and disadvantages of using different mediums (e.g., print or digital text, video, multimedia) to present a particular topic or idea. Analyze a case in which two or more texts provide conflicting information on the same topic and identify where the texts disagree on matters of fact or interpretation. By the end of the year, read and comprehend literary nonfiction in the grades 6–8 text complexity band proficiently, with scaffolding as needed at the high end of the range.	**Reading Standards for Informational Text** Analyze various accounts of a subject told in different mediums (e.g., a person's life story in both print and multimedia), determining which details are emphasized in each account. Analyze seminal U.S. documents of historical and literary significance (e.g., Washington's Farewell Address, the Gettysburg Address, Roosevelt's Four Freedoms speech, King's "Letter from Birmingham Jail"), including how they address related themes and concepts. By the end of grade 9, read and comprehend literary nonfiction in the grades 9–10 text complexity band proficiently, with scaffolding as needed at the high end of the range. By the end of grade 10, read and comprehend literary nonfiction at the high end of the grades 9–10 text complexity band independently and proficiently.

Conclusion

Taking the first step toward content area collaborations to find authentic and engaging nonfiction texts to use in the language arts classroom is the hard part; the actual collaboration benefits both teachers and students! It's time to take some action . . .

Action Steps

1. Three models for collaborating with content area colleagues were presented in this chapter: informational text-based units, Nonfiction Fridays, and the Cross-Content Area Reading Framework. Which framework works best for you? Why?

   _____

   _____

   _____

   _____

2. Sketch out a plan for using content area topic in your classroom using the model you chose above:

   a. Informational text-based unit:

   b. Nonfiction Fridays:

   c. Content Area Reading Framework (template provided at end of chapter):

Works Cited

Anderson, L. A. (2010). *Chains*. New York: Atheneum.

Benjamin, A. (2007). *But I'm not a reading teacher!* New York: Routledge.

Gallagher, K. (2009). *Readicide: How schools are killing reading and what you can do about it.* New York: Stenhouse.

Gehrke, N. J. (1998). A look at curriculum integration from the bridge. *The Curriculum Journal, 9*, 247–260.

Haddon, M. (2003). *The curious incident of the dog in the night-time.* New York: Knopf.

Kelly, J. (2011). *The evolution of Calpurnia Tate.* New York: Squarefish.

National Governors Association for Best Practices, Council of Chief State School Officers. (2011). Common core state standards (English language arts). Washington, DC: Author.

Quick, M. (2012). *Boy 21*. Boston: Little, Brown.

Vacca, J., Vacca, R., & Mraz, M. (2013). *Content area reading: Literacy and learning across the curriculum*. New York: Pearson.

Template 5.1 Cross-content Area Reading Framework

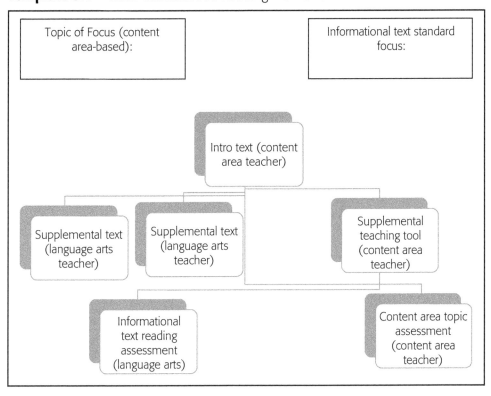

Copyright 2014 Taylor & Francis. All rights reserved. www.routledge.com

Work with Students to Develop Strategies to Cite Evidence When Working with All Texts

I had thought I had done a good job introducing textual evidence to a group of sixth graders. We had gone through an explanation of what it was, done a few sample questions together, and modeled looking back in the text again and again for support for responses. However, Jacob's answer to a question about a text we had read in class about global warming showed otherwise. When asked to find textual evidence to support the claim that the earth's temperature was rising, he wrote, "The evidence is in my brain, and the brain of my neighbor." I obviously needed to go over it again.

Why Is This Item on the List So Important?

The use of textual evidence to support reasoning is not just an informational text goal; it must be a goal for students to use textual evidence to support thinking in responses to reading and in writing (CCSS, 2011). As early as Grade 3, students are asked to refer back to the text as the basis for answers.

Many teachers feel that they are already accomplishing this with students by asking the follow-up question, "How do you know this?" However, this question opens the door to use a citation like Jacob's above. The most simple and basic way to get students to begin to always use textual evidence in responses is by tweaking that question slightly: "What evidence from the text supports that idea?"

Since the Common Core State Standards were released, the biggest complaint I hear from teachers in conjunction with this standard is the same from the early grades through high school: Getting students to look back in the text for evidence to support reasoning is not something that comes naturally or something that they have any desire to do. We must therefore craft experiences in our classrooms where finding and referring to textual evidence in discussion and writing is as natural as breathing.

> Do this—not that principle #6: DO work with students to develop strategies to cite evidence when working with all texts. DON'T allow students to address text topics without being held accountable for using evidence.

To Get Started

Requiring students to use textual evidence to support an opinion or a response during discussion and writing levels the playing field in classrooms where background knowledge and experience varies. Think about it: If you are reading something about a beach, students who have visited the beach will bring a wealth of knowledge to the table before even reading the first line. They can describe what the sand feels like, the noise of seagulls flying overhead—their synapses are firing! It is only natural for a reader to begin responding to a text by trying to make connections, usually personal ones (Rosenblatt, 2005). But for a student without those experiences, his or her background knowledge is being shaped by the text being read. Therefore, I believe in inviting students to share personal responses and connections, first, as a way into the text, but ceasing those conversations before they take over the entire class period. Allowing students to rely solely on their background knowledge in discussion and writing will put them at a disadvantage in situations of close reading and writing about texts. By instead saying, "We will use this text today to drive our discussion," you are inviting everyone into the conversation, entering on equal footing.

This is easier said than done. I sat in on a discussion of Plato's "The Cave" recently. The teacher was excited to show what sophisticated conversation his ninth graders could have on such a complex text. His questions went like this:

"Do you believe experience trumps classroom learning?"
"What other ideas have been influenced by this writing?"
"Describe other 'caves' in modern life in which people might be imprisoned or feel imprisoned."

The conversation was rich, but, at the end of the period, I had not counted a single instance where a student even felt the need to reference the text or use textual evidence to support a point.

Instructional Practices to Update

Updated Strategy #1: Using New Bloom's Taxonomy Question Stems to Produce Text-Dependent Questions

When beginning the practice of requiring students to use textual evidence to support their responses, the best place to start is with your own instruction, specifically your questioning techniques. Questioning is what teachers *do*; we use questions to keep students engaged in learning, to check for understanding, and for formative and summative assessment (Marzano, Pickering, & Pollock, 2001). Textbooks and other prepared curriculum materials hinge upon the questions provided that teachers can use with their students.

There are two types of questions that teachers generally ask in the classroom: Interrogative and connective. Interrogative questions take a "sage on the stage" stance—I am the expert and you will tell me what you know (Wilen, Ishler, & Hutchinson, 2000). They rarely require a student to dig deep into a text to support their responses. One teacher, upon examining the questions provided by her anthology, exclaimed, "They are all surface-level questions!" They checked for comprehension, that was all. The other questions, connective, don't require the students to use the text at all; they often start with question stems like "How would you feel . . .?" "What would you do . . .?" or "What do you think . . .?" The questions provided by the teacher on the Plato text are all connective questions—they are effective at getting students into a discussion about the text topic but do not require them to use the text at all to participate.

To meet the shift in the Common Core that requires students to use textual evidence, we need to change our questioning practices. It is easy to turn to our friend Benjamin Bloom, who developed his taxonomy to clearly delineate the types of questions and instructional practices we use in the classroom (Bloom, 1956). An adaption of Bloom's Taxonomy with question stems for nonfiction text is shown in Table 6.1.

Table 6.1 Bloom's Taxonomy with Sample Question Stems for Nonfiction

Level	Question Stems
Knowledge	What happened after . . .? Name the . . . Find the meaning of . . . Which is true or false . . .?
Comprehension	What was the main idea . . .? Who was the key character . . .? Distinguish between . . .
Application	Describe another instance where . . . Could this have happened in . . .? What factors should change if . . .? Would this information be useful if . . . had a . . .?
Analysis	How was this similar to . . .? What was the underlying theme of . . .? What was the turning point . . .? How is . . . similar to . . .?
Synthesis	Plan an alternative ending to . . . Propose a new solution to . . . Predict . . . based on . . .
Evaluation	Is there a better solution to . . .? How effective are . . .? Is . . . a good or bad solution to . . .? What changes to . . . are necessary for . . . to occur?
After all of the questions above, be sure to also ask: ***What evidence in the text supports this idea?***	

You will notice in Table 6.1 the complete absence of the word "you." An emphasis in text-dependent questioning lies in the students writing about the text without putting themselves "in" the text, e.g., "I think . . ." or "My opinion is . . . ." Questions that tap into these kinds of answers, also known as "On My Own Questions" from the Question-Answer Relationship Strategy, can lead to students not using the text to help support their answer (Raphael & Au, 2005). To get students to use text-based evidence, get into the habit of not asking questions that prompt the student to answer with "I think," but instead with "The text says . . . ."

A key idea in using question stems like the ones above is that some of the spontaneity in questioning your students about a text they have read has to be set aside until you feel that you have mastered the art of text-dependent questioning. Before reading a text with students, it is advisable to plan out a set of text-dependent questions to use to ensure that you are continuing to lead students back to the text for their answers; it is easy to fall back into the connective or interrogative trap when your questions are not clearly laid out!

Updated Strategy #2: Planning a Set of Text-Dependent Questions

Now that we have dabbled in Bloom's, let's get down to the nitty-gritty of writing a set of text-dependent questions. A fantastic website, www.achievethecore.org (Achieve the Core, 2013), developed an entire module on producing and evaluating text-dependent questions—I have modified the plan presented there to fit the needs and ideas of nonfiction text.

Let's start with a text. Figure 6.1 contains the preamble of the Constitution, a weighty, complex text if there ever was one!

Figure 6.1 Preamble of the Constitution

We the People of the United States, in Order to form a more perfect Union, establish Justice, insure domestic Tranquility, provide for the common defense, promote the general Welfare, and secure the Blessings of Liberty to ourselves and our Posterity, do ordain and establish this Constitution for the United States of America.

Step One: Identifying a focus for instruction. To even begin to develop a set of text-dependent questions, I must read the text closely and decide what my focus for instruction in conjunction with this text will be: comprehension (Reading Informational Text, Standards 2–3), author's craft (Reading Informational Text, Standards 4–6), or integration/comparison (Reading Informational Text, Standards 7–9). I know that Reading Informational Text, Standard 1, using textual evidence to support my responses and Reading Informational Text, Standard 10, read and respond to a variety of complex texts, will always be in play, so I can narrow my focus down to the remaining eight standards. In rereading the Preamble, I feel that the vocabulary is key to students truly understanding it, as the authors selected words that may not be in common usage today. Therefore, the author's craft of word choice will be the instructional focus of this text.

Step Two: A way in question. As stated earlier, when we first read a text, we are searching for connections, trying to make sense of the meaning using our background knowledge. Denying this connection to text is not natural; instead we need to acknowledge it with a question or two that draws the reader in without dwelling on these connections too long. I want to encourage connections to engage any background knowledge that a student may have. A way in question with this text may be as simple as: "Where have you seen this text before?" I might follow it up with, "A clue is in the last line about where it comes from. Put your finger on that clue."

Step Three: Honing in on the instructional focus. As I decided that author's craft, particularly word choice, impacts this text greatly, I will next lead students in that direction. My next question would be: "Is this a formal or informal text? What evidence from the text supports this opinion?" This question allows students to begin to think about the writing itself while also forcing them back to the text to provide the evidence necessary for true text-dependent questioning. I would then follow up that question with, "What words in the text lend a sense of formality to the text? How do they contribute to the overall tone?"

Step Four: Application/Synthesis/Evaluation. The final question should actually be the lead-in to the higher level work that students will do with the instructional focus. Now that we have examined the text closely and reread it a few times to delve deep into author's craft, students are ready to try out this strategy themselves. My next instructions would be: "The architects of the Preamble to the Constitution chose words to clearly express the ideals of our Founding Fathers. However, many people today find the Preamble to be hard to understand because of some of the archaic language used. Keeping word choice in mind, with a partner, rewrite the Preamble using language appropriate to today's teenager. You may use a dictionary or thesaurus to aid you in the quest to rewrite the Preamble." All prior questioning leads up to this—the point at which students apply the instructional focus to the text.

Using these types of questions and questioning sequences in the classroom leads to the type of close reading that has been buzzed about with the Common Core State Standards (Boyles, 2012/2013). However, the rereading doesn't feel tedious or over-blown; students are naturally going back to the text to respond to the questions. The amount of text is another piece to consider. I used *a sentence* to compose this set of questions—a complex and important sentence but a sentence, nonetheless. Using short excerpts like this one helps students to dive into a text without feeling overwhelmed. Later, as students (and you!) grow proficient at responding and working with these types of questions, the excerpts and stories can grow.

Figure 6.2 lays out the steps to creating text-dependent questioning (a template of this graphic is included at the end of the chapter).

Figure 6.2   Steps to Create a Set of Text-dependent Questions

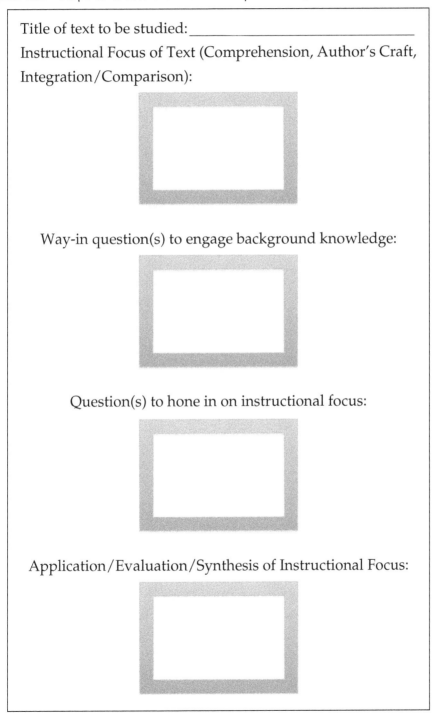

Title of text to be studied: _____

Instructional Focus of Text (Comprehension, Author's Craft, Integration/Comparison):

Way-in question(s) to engage background knowledge:

Question(s) to hone in on instructional focus:

Application/Evaluation/Synthesis of Instructional Focus:

Updated Strategy #3: Using a Graphic Organizer to Assist Students in Organizing Their Textual Evidence for Discussion and Writing

Okay, so we have now tweaked our basic classroom questioning about text and learned how to develop a sequence of questions relating to text. Our final strategy is for the students, a graphic organizer. In my response to that initial complaint from teachers about students' lack of motivation to go back to the text to find textual evidence to support their ideas, I began to develop a basic graphic organizer to scaffold this thinking. This graphic organizer, shown in Figure 6.3, was developed explicitly for Reading Informational Text, Standard 2: Determine the main idea(s) of a text and show how it is supported by key details.

Figure 6.3 Textual Evidence Graphic Organizer

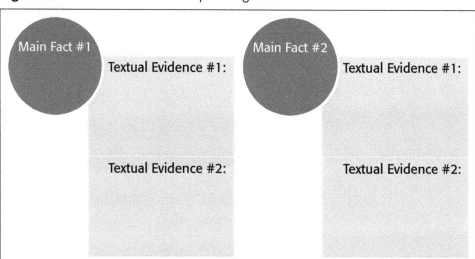

The success with this graphic organizer is best explained by an actual student. Jamiah, a ninth grader, stated, "I had to go back into the text to support what I thought was the main idea of the text. I liked there was a place to put my support."

As with any graphic organizer, this cannot be the end product of using textual evidence. This graphic organizer was made to be turned into a short writing piece, with a student stating the main facts presented in an article and the textual evidence supporting those main facts. Figure 6.4 shows a filled out Textual Evidence Graphic Organizer on an article about oil fracking along with a summary paragraph written by a seventh grade student using the graphic organizer for support.

Figure 6.4 Completed Textual Evidence Graphic Organizer with Student Writing

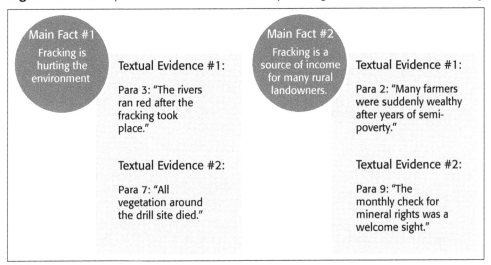

The article, "Is fracking a good thing for Ohio?" presents two main ideas to the reader. It first presents the idea that fracking is hurting the environment. The author supports this idea by mentioning that "The river ran red after the fracking took place," showing that the fracking had caused something bad on the land. This idea is also supported by the line, "All vegetation around the drill site died," which shows that the drill caused plants to die. A second idea presented in the article is that fracking is a source of income for many rural landowners. This idea is supported by the fact that "Many farmers were suddenly wealthy after years of semi-poverty." It is also supported by the fact that "The monthly check for mineral rights was a welcome sight." Both these lines show that fracking contributes to the income of the farmers.

Common Core Connection

The strategies presented above fit well with two specific standards in the Common Core State Standards for English Language Arts and are presented in Figure 6.5.

Figure 6.5 Common Core State Standards Addressed in this Chapter

Grade Level	4	5	6
Standard Addressed	**Reading Standards for Informational Text** Refer to details and examples in a text when explaining what the text says explicitly and when drawing inferences from a text. Determine the main idea of a text and explain how it is supported by key details; summarize the text.	**Reading Standards for Informational Text** Quote accurately from a text when explaining what the text says explicitly and when drawing inferences from the text. Determine two or more main ideas of a text and explain how they are supported by key details; summarize the text.	**Reading Standards for Informational Text** Cite textual evidence to support analysis of what the text says explicitly as well as inferences drawn from the text. Determine a central idea of a text and how it is conveyed through particular details; provide a summary of the text distinct from personal opinions or judgments.

Grade Level	7	8	9–10
Standard Addressed	**Reading Standards for Informational Text** Cite several pieces of textual evidence to support analysis of what the text says explicitly as well as inferences drawn from the text. Determine two or more central ideas in a text and analyze their development over the course of the text; provide an objective summary of the text.	**Reading Standards for Informational Text** Cite the textual evidence that most strongly supports an analysis of what the text says explicitly as well as inferences drawn from the text. Determine a central idea of a text and analyze its development over the course of the text, including its relationship to supporting ideas; provide an objective summary of the text.	**Reading Standards for Informational Text** Cite strong and thorough textual evidence to support analysis of what the text says explicitly as well as inferences drawn from the text. Determine a central idea of a text and analyze its development over the course of the text, including how it emerges and is shaped and refined by specific details; provide an objective summary of the text.

Conclusion

Getting students to cite textual evidence while reading is not easy, but attainable! It is time to take some action . . .

Action Steps

1. Start by looking at a set of questions that came with a textbook or text that you use in the classroom. Analyze these questions; do they fall into the higher or lower categories of Bloom's Taxonomy? Do they really require students to go back into the text to fully answer the question?

   _____

   _____

   _____

   _____

2. Rewrite one of the questions you reviewed above to make it more text dependent. Write your new, revised question here:

   _____

   _____

   _____

3. Time to develop a set of text-dependent questions on your own! Select a text worthy of study. Then, using the text-dependent question development steps, write a series of questions:

   a. Way in question(s):

      _____

      _____

   b. Instructional focus question(s):

      _____

      _____

   c. Application/Synthesis/Evaluation of Instructional Focus:

      _____

      _____

      _____

      _____

Works Cited

Achieve the Core. (2013). Text dependent question resources. Retrieved October 28, 2013, from www.achievethecore.org/page/710/text-dependent-question-resources

Bloom, B. (1956). *Taxonomy of educational objectives: The classification of educational goals, Handbook I: Cognitive domain.* New York: Longman Green.

Boyles, N. (2012/2013). Closing in on close reading. *Educational Leadership, 70,* 36–41.

Marzano, R., Pickering, D., & Pollock, J. (2001). *Classroom instruction that works: Research-based strategies for increasing student achievement.* Alexandria, VA: Association for Supervision and Curriculum Development.

National Governors Association for Best Practices, Council of Chief State School Officers. (2011). Common core state standards (English Language Arts). Washington, DC: Author.

Raphael, T., & Au, K. (2005). Enhancing comprehension and test taking across grades and content areas. *The Reading Teacher, 59,* 206–221.

Rosenblatt, L. (2005). *Making meaning with text: Selected essays.* Portsmouth, NH: Heinemann.

Wilen, W., Ishler, M., & Hutchinson, J. (2000). *Dynamics of teaching.* New York: Longman.

Template 6.1 Steps to Create a Set of Text-dependent Questions

Title of text to be studied:_____

Instructional Focus of Text (Comprehension, Author's Craft, Integration/Comparison):

Way-in question(s) to engage background knowledge:

Question(s) to hone in on instructional focus:

Application/Evaluation/Synthesis of instructional focus:

Copyright 2014 Taylor & Francis. All rights reserved. www.routledge.com

Template 6.2   Textual Evidence Graphic Organizer

Name:

Date:

Article/text(s):

Textual Evidence Organizer
After reading, come up with two main facts from the article/text. Then find two incidents of textual evidence (proof from the article) that back up your two main facts.

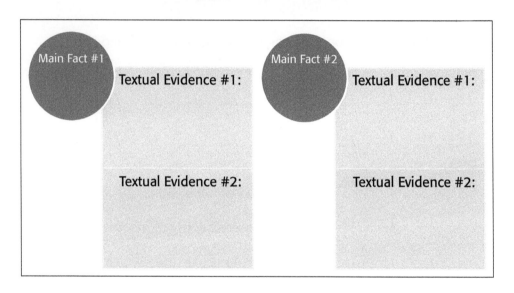

Copyright 2014 Taylor & Francis. All rights reserved. www.routledge.com

Create and Scaffold Varied and Interesting Nonfiction Writing Assignments that Range from Informal to Formal, Depending on Purpose

At each desk sat a stack of blank notecards. "What are these?" I asked the teacher prepping for the lesson. She walked over to one and let them sift through her fingers like playing cards. "It's time to start our research reports," she said. "By the time we are done, each one of these cards will have a fact on them from a resource that we have researched." "How many facts must they have?" I responded, feeling the heft of the stack. "At least 50," she replied. "That is how I am stepping up the rigor of informational writing—more facts."

Why Is This Item on the List So Important?

Did that anecdote above give you flashbacks to the "term paper" you wrote in high school? Stacks of notecards, organized by topic—that is how many of us learned to write informational text papers, and it is the legacy that we pass on to today's students, despite the numerous developments in research tools (hello, Internet, goodbye microfiche!), writing tools (a bibliography creator is the new student best friend), and writing forms (tweets, anyone?). I do not deny that there is a place for the "big" research project; writing an extended paper on a topic is excellent preparation for some of the types of writing that students may need to do as part of their college experiences and future careers. However, we need to realize that it is not the only type of informational writing out there. In fact, the majority of the writing our students will end up doing for their future jobs will be product proposals, productivity summaries, recommendations, and more—all of the shorter variety. One CEO from a well-known company actually pleaded with educators to work with students on writing professional emails, tweets, and memos, citing the lack of "respect and restraint" in the communication she received with young hires in her company.

This chapter is not going to be a "how-to" on the big research report. Instead, it will focus on interesting, engaging ways to conduct short research projects that result in informational and argumentative texts in response to the reading of nonfiction texts in the language arts classroom.

> Do this—not that principle #7: DO create and scaffold varied and interesting nonfiction writing assignments that range from informal to formal, depending on purpose. DON'T assign only one or two major writing projects throughout the year with little time for the writing process to occur.

To Get Started

To open yourself up to the ideas in this chapter, you are going to have to let go of the traditional, multi-paragraph essay. Like the research project, the five paragraph essay has its place; it is one form of writing that teachers have traditionally used as a formula for teaching writing, especially preparing students for the type of writing that appears on standardized tests (Johnson, Thompson, Smagorinsky, & Fry, 2003; Wesley, 2000). The criticism of the five paragraph essay exists in the fact that students often concentrate more on the form (getting the information into an introduction, conclusion, and three supporting paragraphs) than on the content they are trying to express (Johnson et al., 2003; Simmons, 2005; Wesley, 2000). Bottom line: Teach the five paragraph essay as one form of writing; allow other writing experiences in your classroom to truly prepare students for college and career writing.

One important point of emphasis in this chapter is the use of mentor texts to instigate informational writing. Mentor texts can be powerful tools to show students the possibilities in writing (Dorfman & Capelli, 2007, 2009; Fletcher 2011). Each new type of informational writing that is scaffolded in the classroom should be introduced with a mentor text, an excellent example of the kind of writing that students will be asked to do. For example, if students will be asked to write an argument in tweets, they need to examine good tweets to see what they should include and what they should discard.

Updated Strategy #1: Multigenre Response: Using Informal
Writing Formats for Nonfiction Reading and Writing

Tom Romano has written extensively on the use of multigenre papers and projects as an alternative to the traditional five paragraph essay (2000). His whole approach asks teachers to allow students to use their imaginations in responding to research they have read or new ideas they have encountered by creating a set number of genres that show their new learning.

He begins this kind of research by having students turn their topic into a research question: for example, if you are studying the life of Martin Luther King, Jr., the question might be "Who was MLK?" Reading and research takes place; the student documents where they are learning this information in a traditional works cited page, keeping track of the facts learned in a variety of ways (if you can't part from your notecards like in the anecdote above, this is the place for them). Finally, students "show what they know" by expressing their new knowledge in a variety of genres, the number being set by the teacher. Figure 7.1 lists a small set of possible genres that students could use in their multigenre project.

Figure 7.1   Possible Genres for a Multigenre Project

Tweets	Editorial	Rant
Emails	Driver's license	Series of texts
Marriage license	Wedding announcement	Journal entries
Recipe	Tattoo	Blurb
Shopping list	Interview	Play
Graffiti	Greeting card	Contract
Wanted poster	Resume	Song
Job application	Ad	Epitaph

Multigenre projects can be grand (10 genres or more, a set number of required resources, etc.) or quite informal. In a fourth grade social studies class, we used multigenre writing to see what students had learned about their home state, Ohio. We did all the research together; read from the textbook and several picture books, investigated websites, and looked at pictures from the state's history. Students were then asked to select three genres to use to express their learning. We limited the list from Figure 7.1 to make it more fourth grader friendly (Figure 7.2).

Figure 7.2 Fourth Grade-friendly List of Possible Genres

| Recipe | Song | Ad |
| Greeting card | Series of texts | Email |

Students worked with a partner to create these genres. To document the new knowledge behind the genre, Romano (2000) uses what he calls a "Notespage." This notespage can be used in addition to a works cited page; to me, it is what sets apart a multigenre project from traditional writing. After each genre, students write a paragraph, detailing where they found the actual facts for the text they created, describing the creative and research process behind the writing. An example from the fourth grade Ohio history multigenre project can be found in Figure 7.3, along with the notespage entry that accompanied it.

Figure 7.3 Sample Ohio History Multigenre Project

RECIPE FOR A GREAT STATE

Ingredients:

One Great Lake
Several important rivers
Three major cities
A border war with neighbors to the north
Rolling hills in the south
Farmland

Directions: Place the Great Lake to the north of the state. Have the Cuyahoga river empty into it. Place the Ohio River at the south end of the state, defining the border. Sprinkle Cleveland, Columbus, and Cincinnati through the center of the state. Have one border war with Michigan to see who gets Toledo. Finally, spread rolling hills through the southern part of the state and farmland all over.

Notespage: We wrote this recipe after reading about Ohio geography in our history textbook. We learned about the major features of Ohio and thought they would make a good recipe.

Mentor texts in a multigenre project are interesting; they are not traditional children's books or articles (although, they can be, if those are genres you will allow students to use!). I have found it helpful to have an example, or mentor text, of each genre in my "possible genre list" so that students cannot only learn about the form (epitaph is always a popular one but few students know what it is!) but can see how it might look once written. It takes a bit of time to pull these together, but having a binder or station of these set up in the classroom helps students to see the possibilities in writing in this way.

A few final thoughts on multigenre writing:

♦ There is naturally a lot of choice and differentiation in multigenre writing. Students are working at their own pace, often on genres of their own choosing. Clear due dates and set work times help to manage students on different parts of their projects at different times.

♦ Creating a group multigenre project to help introduce students to the idea of this type of writing is very helpful. I acquired this idea from my colleague, Dr. Alexa Sandmann, who had her students sum up their learning in her course by each picking a course topic and creating a genre to reflect their learning. What resulted was a book of multigenre writing about the entire course. In a K–12 classroom, after studying a particular topic, students could pick a sub-topic or idea that appealed to them and contribute a genre to a class book.

♦ And, if you still feel the need for a five paragraph essay, make it a required genre for the multigenre project!

Updated Strategy #2: Letters, Brochures, Speeches, and More: Using Formal Writing Formats for Argumentative Reading and Writing

Multigenre writing clearly addressed informational writing; using research to produce informative pieces. Letters, brochures, and speeches are all forms of writing that can be used for informational writing, too, but lend themselves beautifully to formal opinion/argumentative writing. Argumentative writing has been noted as another key shift in the Common Core State Standards (Calkins, Ehrenworth, & Lehman, 2012). The ability to create logical reasoning on the behalf of an issue begins with opinion writing in grades K–5 and transitions to argumentative writing in grades 6–12. Again, a five paragraph essay would suffice here, but allowing students to express their opinions in letters, brochures, and speeches allows them to stretch their writing legs beyond the confines of traditional writing. These formats give students a sense of audience, a "who" behind the reader.

The RAFT strategy is a great place to help students plan writing with audience in mind. In this strategy, students use a graphic organizer to think about their role as the writer (R), the audience or recipient of the writing (A), the format the writing will take place in (F), and the topic that will be addressed (Dean, 2006; Santa, Havens, & Valdes, 2004). Table 7.1 presents a blank RAFT graphic organizer (a blank template is presented at the end of the chapter).

Table 7.1   RAFT Graphic Organizer

Role	Audience	Format	Topic

In many cases with the RAFT, the teacher assigns one of the four categories, i.e., "your role in writing this text will be a parent questioning homework practices at the school," or "the format of your writing will be a letter." However, as students grow proficient at matching their writing up to the appropriate role, audience, format, and topic, this graphic organizer helps them define their writing. I know many teachers who will not allow their students to begin a new writing piece without completing a RAFT first to "float" their writing to success! Table 7.2 presents a completed RAFT graphic organizer by a sixth grader. His class had just finished reading about the pros and cons of having cell phones allowed in schools. The teacher designated the topic: cell phones in the school. The rest was up to him:

Table 7.2   Completed RAFT Graphic Organizer

Role	Audience	Format	Topic
Expert on the use of cell phones in instruction	Teachers at Milkovich Middle School	Brochure	Cell phones in schools

As you can see, this student used this graphic organizer to set up his role as one in favor of cell phones in schools. He ended up having to do research on the use of cell phones in instruction and presented his information in a brochure that was so good, the teacher presented it at a faculty meeting!

Resources for mentor texts. Just as with multigenre writing, mentor texts for formal argumentative writing that goes beyond traditional paragraphs is not always something that can be turned up in a textbook or writing handbook. I have a gathered a few great resources to scaffold the reading and writing of such forms in Table 7.3.

Table 7.3 Resources for Mentor Texts to Write Letters, Brochures, and Speeches

Letters	1. *Postcards from Pluto* (Leedy, 2006). This adorable picture book shows the possibilities in using letters (or postcards in this case) to showcase new knowledge on a nonfiction topic.
	2. *Sincerely yours: Writing your own letters* (Lowen, 2009). Introduces both friendly and business letter formats.
	3. **Compilation of letters to the editor:** www.asatonline. org/forum/archives/time/time
	This fascinating resource presents an article published in *Time Magazine* on autism. Included are several letters that readers wrote in response, arguing for or against the validity of the article.
Brochures	1. **Lesson plan:** www.readwritethink.org/classroom-resources/lesson-plans/brochures-writing-audience-purpose-1002.html. This resource has daily lesson plans to scaffold brochure writing with students in grades 9–12.
	2. **Museum and hotel lobbies**. Let me explain—when you walk into most museums and hotel lobbies, there is usually a stand of brochures available to let guests know about attractions in the area. Grab a handful!
Speeches	1. From the History Channel, a link to the transcript and audio of over 300 famous speeches: www.history.com/speeches
	2. Another link to a set of lesson plans that help students analyze great speeches as arguments: www.readwritethink.org/classroom-resources/lesson-plans/analyzing-famous-speeches

Common Core Connection

The strategies presented above fit well with the writing anchor standards on informational and opinion/argumentative writing in the Common Core State Standards for English Language Arts, which are presented in Figure 7.4.

Figure 7.4 Common Core State Standards Addressed in this Chapter

Grade Level	4	5	6
Standard Addressed	**Writing Standards** Write opinion pieces on topics or texts, supporting a point of view with reasons and information. Write informative/explanatory texts to examine a topic and convey ideas and information clearly. Conduct short research projects that build knowledge through investigation of different aspects of a topic.	**Writing Standards** Write opinion pieces on topics or texts, supporting a point of view with reasons and information. Write informative/explanatory texts to examine a topic and convey ideas and information clearly. Conduct short research projects that use several sources to build knowledge through investigation of different aspects of a topic.	**Writing Standards** Write arguments to support claims with clear reasons and relevant evidence. Write informative/explanatory texts to examine a topic and convey ideas, concepts, and information through the selection, organization, and analysis of relevant content. Conduct short research projects to answer a question, drawing on several sources and refocusing the inquiry when appropriate.
Grade Level	7	8	9–10
Standard Addressed	**Writing Standards** Write arguments to support claims with clear reasons and relevant evidence. Write informative/explanatory texts to examine a topic and convey ideas, concepts, and information through the selection, organization, and analysis of relevant content. Conduct short research projects to answer a question, drawing on several sources and generating additional related, focused questions for further research and investigation.	**Writing Standards** Write arguments to support claims with clear reasons and relevant evidence. Write informative/explanatory texts to examine a topic and convey ideas, concepts, and information through the selection, organization, and analysis of relevant content. Conduct short research projects to answer a question (including a self-generated question), drawing on several sources and generating additional related, focused questions that allow for multiple avenues of exploration.	**Writing Standards** Write arguments to support claims in an analysis of substantive topics or texts, using valid reasoning and relevant and sufficient evidence. Write informative/explanatory texts to examine and convey complex ideas, concepts, and information clearly and accurately through the effective selection, organization, and analysis of content. Conduct short as well as more sustained research projects to answer a question (including a self-generated question) or solve a problem; narrow or broaden the inquiry when appropriate; synthesize multiple sources on the subject, demonstrating understanding of the subject under investigation.

Conclusion

Writing engaging, authentic informational and opinion/argumentative pieces can be fun for you and your students! It is time to take some action . . .

Action Steps

1. Design a multigenre writing experience for your students. Scaffold this first multigenre experience with a shared end product. What topic will everyone study and write about?

   _____

   _____

2. Put together a list of possible genres for students to use to "show what they know."

   _____

   _____

   _____

   _____

3. Create a model RAFT graphic organizer to use when introducing the students to the strategy. Have students fill out their own RAFT graphic organizer before writing an argumentative piece. Did it help clarify their writing? Why or why not?

   _____

   _____

Works Cited

Calkins, L., Ehrenworth, M., & Lehman, C. (2012). *Pathways to the Common Core: Accelerating achievement*. Portsmouth, NH: Heinemann.

Dean, D. (2006). *Strategic writing: The writing process and beyond in the secondary English classroom*. Urbana, IL: NCTE.

Dorfman, L., & Capelli, R. (2007). *Mentor texts: Teaching writing through children's literature, K-6*. Portland, ME: Stenhouse.

Dorfman, L., & Capelli, R. (2009). *Nonfiction mentor texts: Teaching informational writing through children's literature, K-8*. Portland, ME: Stenhouse.

Fletcher, R. (2011). *Mentor author, mentor texts: Short texts, craft notes and practical classroom uses*. Portsmouth, NH: Heinemann.

Johnson, T., Thompson, L., Smagorinsky, P., & Fry, P. (2003). Learning to teach the five-paragraph theme. *Research in the Teaching of English, 38*, 136–175.

Romano, T. (2000). *Blending genre, altering style: Writing multigenre papers*. Portsmouth, NH: Heinemann.

Santa, C., Havens, L., & Valdes, B. (2004). *Project Criss: Creating independence through student-owned strategies*. Dubuque, IA: Kendall Hunt.

Simmons, J. (2005). Improving writing for college: The conditions to do it well. *The English Journal, 94*, 75–80.

Wesley, K. (2000). The ill effects of the five paragraph theme. *English Journal, 90*, 57–60.

Template 7.1 RAFT Graphic Organizer

Name: _____

Date: _____

Role	Audience	Format	Topic

Copyright 2014 Taylor & Francis. All rights reserved. www.routledge.com

Use Text Structure as Both a Reading and Writing Tool to Assist Students in Analyzing Any Nonfiction Text

"Today we are going to talk about the different text structures that nonfiction authors use in their writing," I announced to a group of eighth graders. A collective groan went up from the group. I paused before turning to the Smartboard and asked, "What's the matter?" Hands flew in the air. "Dr. Wilfong, no offense," Taylor said, "but we learn this every year." "But on the pretest, you all only knew one text structure well enough to identify it," I replied, gesturing to the pile of entrance slips on the table. "Well," Jose continued, speaking on behalf of the class, "we learned about it but it is obviously not important enough to remember for next year."

Why Is This Item on the List So Important?

Text structure is vital to student comprehension of nonfiction text (Dymock & Nicholson, 2010; Read, Reutzel, & Fawson, 2008; Shanahan, Fisher, & Frey, 2012). Good readers use schema to help make sense of new things they are learning; in informational text, a schema that students tap into could be the organization or structure of that text. Teaching text structure has been shown to boost comprehension of nonfiction text in English Language Learners and students diagnosed with a learning disability (Dreher & Gray, 2009; Gaddy, Bakken, & Fulk, 2008; Li-Hao, Schwartz, & Baule, 2011).

And, judging from the anecdote above, text structure is something we *have* been teaching—year after year, possibly in similar ways—but for several reasons, the information is not sticking with students (or, as Jose put it, it is not "important enough" to remember).

In kindergarten through third grade, students are asked to use "text features" to help them locate information in the text: captions, headings, key words, sidebars, etc. (CCSS, 2011). But starting in fourth grade, students are asked to describe the text structure of an informational text; in fifth grade, they take that knowledge of text structure and use it to compare how two texts describe the same idea or event. This grows over the years until students are able to analyze how sections, sentences, and paragraphs contribute to the organization of an author's claims and evidence. Simply being able to identify text structure is not enough; students need to know why and how an author uses text structure to organize their writing.

> **Do this—not that principle #8: DO use text structure as both a reading and writing tool to assist students in analyzing any nonfiction text; DON'T teach text structure in isolation.**

To Get Started

Identification of different text structures and their signal words is the first step for students when it comes to working with nonfiction text. And, as stated above, the big teaching of text structure should take place in fourth grade with a reminder (brief!) in the following grades as students get prepared to do more sophisticated work with text structure and informational text. But, as we are all realizing, the switch to the Common Core will not happen overnight; it will behoove all teachers to give an in-depth review of text structure for the next couple of years beyond fourth grade to close any gaps in the switch from individual state standards to the Common Core State Standards.

It is helpful to start with a shared definition of what text structure is exactly. Text structure is "a mental awareness of how writers organize information" (Dymock & Nicholson, 2010, p. 168). Share this definition with students; in my own instruction of this topic, I often skipped the *why* we were learning this. Before I share the *what* of text structure (the types, the signal words, the possible graphic organizers), I have to share the purpose of learning text structure: Studying text structure helps the reader think about how an author organizes the information in an article or book (Meyer & Rice, 1984).

When teaching text structure, it is beneficial to distribute a table like the one in Table 8.1. This table gives a basic overview of the different text structures authors can employ when writing, the signal words they might use to show this text structure, and a suggested graphic organizer to help a student take notes from the text in a logical way.

Table 8.1 Text Structure and Signal Words Overview

Text Structure	Associated Graphic Organizer	Signal Words
Descriptive		No specific signal words
Sequence/Chronological		first next second until third while last soon then after at that time now during immediately finally
Compare/Contrast		however even though but on the contrary yet otherwise despite in comparison still on the other hand
Cause & Effect		for this reason thus in order to as a result because consequently so that on account of therefore accordingly
Problem/Solution		problem solution because cause since as a result so that

To teach the identification of text structure, I would recommend presenting one of each type of text at a time, allowing students to explore the characteristic of each type in depth. I like using picture books to do this introduction, giving students space to use their brain power to think about the text structure and not focus on decoding for comprehension. Table 8.2 gives a brief list of my favorite nonfiction picture books to use to introduce expository text structures.

Table 8.2 Nonfiction Picture Books to Introduce Expository Text Structures

Text Type	Suggested Nonfiction Picture Book
Descriptive	Sill, C. (2010). *About Raptors.* Gibbons, G. (1997). *Nature's Green Umbrella.*
Sequence/Chronological	Himmelman, J. (2000). *A House Spider's Life.* Zecca, K. (2007). *A Puffin's Year.* Nelson, V. (2009). *Bad News for Outlaws: The Remarkable Life of Bass Reeves, US Marshall.*
Compare/Contrast	Collard, S. (2008). *Teeth.* Bullard, L. (2010). *What's the Difference Between an Alligator and a Crocodile?*
Cause & Effect	Battan, M. (2003). *Aliens from Earth: When Animals and Plants Invade Other Ecosystems.* Burgan, M. (2012). *Breaker Boys: How a Photograph Helped End Child Labor.*
Problem/Solution	Cherry, L. (2002). *A River Ran Wild.* Patent, D. (2008). *When the Wolves Returned.*

After the initial introduction of the text type, I would begin scaffolding the identification strategy onto more complex texts such as articles and full-length books.

Identification of text type now becomes part of my nonfiction routine: every time we read a nonfiction text, whether as a whole group, in small groups, or even as part of our independent reading, the questions—"What type of text structure is this?" and "What evidence do you have to support that it is that type of text structure?"—will become staple entry points into the text that we can investigate briefly to cement the idea of text structure in my students' minds (and avoid the scenario in the anecdote at the beginning of the chapter). We are now ready to delve deeper into text structure, beyond identification into application and writing!

Updated Strategy #1: Using the Text Structure Think-Mat
to Break Down Informational Text

To take students to the next level in using text structure in reading nonfiction texts, they need to have the ability to break down the text into its parts, not only identifying which text structure is in play but seeing how an author employs the text structure to present information to the reader. These skills will assist students in reaching mastery of this standard in grades 5 and up.

The Text Structure Think-Mat was designed for this purpose. This template was created to help students identify the text structure that is being used and to choose a graphic organizer to break apart the information in the text to analyze the set-up. It is presented in Figure 8.1 and as a template at the end of the chapter.

Figure 8.1 Text Structure Think-Mat

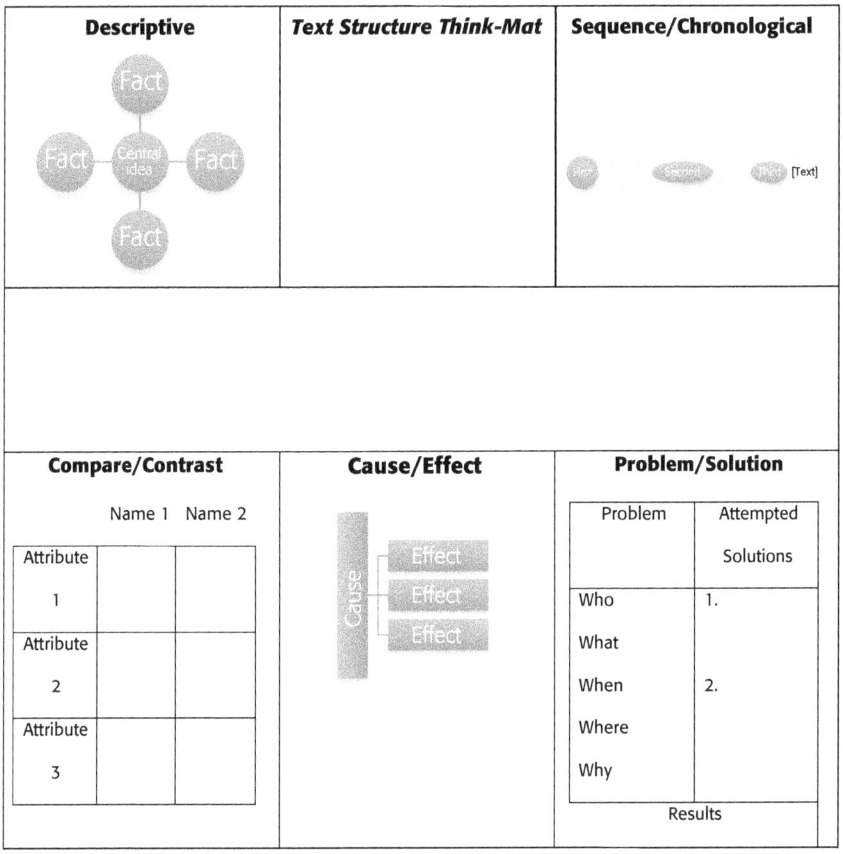

This template can be available to students anytime they read a nonfiction text. As they read, they can keep an eye on their Think-Mat for the structure the author is using to organize their ideas. After reading, they can choose the graphic organizer that best suits the text, re-create it on the center of the Think-Mat, and then fill in the details from the text. From here, students can use this graphic organizer to help think about the decisions the author made setting this text up. Figure 8.2 shows a completed Text Structure Think-Mat, using a text that compared the legacies of Abraham Lincoln and George Washington.

Figure 8.2 Completed Text Structure Think-Mat

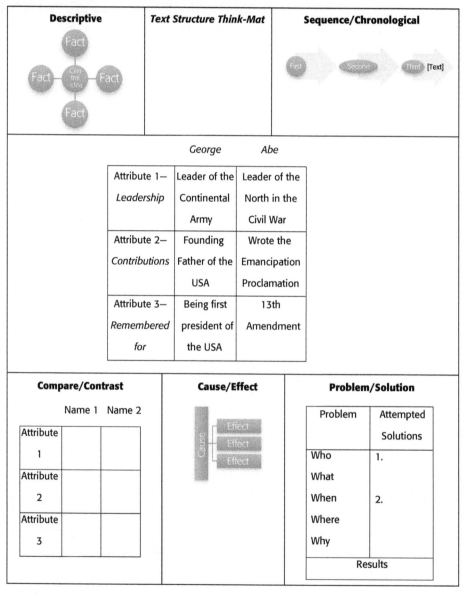

Updated Strategy #2: Using Text Structure as a Writing Tool

The ultimate sophistication in the learning of new knowledge is having the ability to transfer it to your own ideas (Wiggins & McTighe, 2005). Once students can identify text structure, and can break down how an author uses text structure to organize ideas, they are ready to apply these ideas to their own writing. Text structure is not only a reading standard, it is referenced in the informational/expository writing standards; in the introduction of writing their own informational texts, students are supposed to give the reader an idea of the structure being used and then follow through with the structure in the body of their writing.

Copy change. One of the easiest ways to begin to scaffold the use of text structure in writing is copy change. Copy change is a strategy where students employ a framework, usually from a published author, to structure their own writing (Bintz, Wright, & Sheffer, 2010; Rasinski & Padak, 2000). "Professionally borrowing" the author's framework works like training wheels; it gives students the confidence to try something new and a bit difficult and, when they are ready, the framework can be removed, allowing students to write independently.

The Important Book (Brown, 1949), referenced in Chapter 2, is a perfect example of a copy change using the descriptive text structure. Students can borrow Brown's framework to write their own descriptive paragraphs, using the template included in Chapter 2.

Other popular copy change templates for teaching text structure include *If You Give a Mouse a Cookie* (Numeroff, 2010) and *Fortunately, Unfortunately* (Foreman, 2011); both scaffold cause and effect writing. Although these texts are fiction, they work perfectly for students to grasp using text structure in their own, nonfiction writing. A ninth grader used the *If You Give a Mouse a Cookie* template to write her own story entitled, "If You Make a Teenager Get Up Early in the Morning" where she incorporated research about why school should start later. Using the *Fortunately, Unfortunately* template, an eighth grader described the events of the American Revolution. It began:

> Fortunately,
>
> *The American people were ready to work together to fight the British.*
>
> But unfortunately,
>
> *They did not have the resources or training of the British army and it was a hard fought war.*

A template for *Fortunately, Unfortunately* is included in Figure 8.3 and at the end of the chapter.

Figure 8.3   Fortunately, Unfortunately Cause & Effect Copy Change Template

Name _____ # _____

Fortunately . . .

Explain the cause and effect of events using the space below. Fortunately will be the cause and unfortunately will be the effect.

Fortunately,

_____

_____

But unfortunately,

_____

_____

Fortunately,

_____

_____

But unfortunately,

_____

_____

Fortunately,

_____

_____

But unfortunately,

_____

_____

Next steps. After copy change comes independence in writing with text structure. Once the use of text structure becomes a criteria on my rubric for informational or argumentative writing, it needs to be an expectation that students will use their knowledge of text structure to organize their own thoughts. The Text Structure Think-Mat comes back into play here. As a student is planning to write an informational or argumentative piece, the Think-Mat becomes a great place for them to brainstorm how to organize the information logically, using one of the suggested text structures. Figure 8.4 is a completed Text Structure Think-Mat from a seventh grader, who wanted to convince the principal that the cafeteria food needed a serious upgrade. He chose the problem/solution graphic organizer to shape his ideas.

Figure 8.4 Completed Text Structure Think-Mat for Writing

Descriptive	Text Structure Think-Mat	Sequence/Chronological
Fact / Fact–Central idea–Fact / Fact		First Second Third [Text]

Problem	Suggested Solutions
Who 7th graders at Colina Intermediate School	1. The student government could figure out how to work with local farms to get vegetables
What Protesting the quality of cafeteria food	
When Next Friday (unless action is taken)	
Where Outside the cafeteria	
Why Our growing bodies demand fresh, quality ingredients – no more frozen food!	2. We could use the space behind the gym to begin a kitchen garden
Results	
Happy healthy 7th graders! No protest that would surely draw media attention!	

Compare/Contrast

	Name 1	Name 2
Attribute 1		
Attribute 2		
Attribute 3		

Cause/Effect

Cause → Effect / Effect / Effect

Problem/Solution

Problem	Attempted Solutions
Who	1.
What	
When	2.
Where	
Why	
Results	

Two key ideas are at play here. One, it is clear that the student knew which text structure to use for his writing. Two, the student effectively used the graphic organizer to logically organize his ideas (and by the way, the kitchen garden idea was used!).

Common Core Connection

The strategies presented above fit well with several standards in the Common Core State Standards for English Language Arts (see Figure 8.5).

Figure 8.5   Common Core State Standards Addressed in this Chapter

Grade Level	4	5	6
Standard Addressed	**Reading Standards for Informational Text** Describe the overall structure (e.g., chronology comparison, cause/effect, problem/solution) of events, ideas, concepts, or information in a text or part of a text.	**Reading Standards for Informational Text** Compare and contrast the overall structure (e.g., chronology, comparison, cause/effect, problem/solution) of events, ideas, concepts, or information in two or more texts.	**Reading Standards for Informational Text** Analyze how a particular sentence, paragraph, chapter, or section fits into the overall structure of a text and contributes to the development of the ideas.
	Writing Standards *Opinion.* Introduce a topic or text clearly, state an opinion, and create an organizational structure in which related ideas are grouped to support the writer's purpose. *Informational.* Introduce a topic clearly and group related information in paragraphs and sections; include formatting (e.g., headings), illustrations, and multimedia when useful to aiding comprehension.	**Writing Standards** *Opinion.* Introduce a topic or text clearly, state an opinion, and create an organizational structure in which ideas are logically grouped to support the writer's purpose. *Informational.* Introduce a topic clearly, provide a general observation and focus, and group related information logically; include formatting (e.g., headings), illustrations, and multimedia when useful to aiding comprehension.	**Writing Standards** *Argumentative.* Introduce claim(s) and organize the reasons and evidence clearly. *Informational.* Introduce a topic; organize ideas, concepts, and information, using strategies such as definition, classification, comparison/contrast, and cause/effect; include formatting (e.g., headings), graphics (e.g., charts, tables), and multimedia when useful to aiding comprehension.

Grade Level	7	8	9–10

Standard Addressed	**Reading Standards for Informational Text** Analyze the structure an author uses to organize a text, including how the major sections contribute to the whole and to the development of the ideas.
	
	Writing Standards *Argumentative.* Introduce claim(s), acknowledge alternate or opposing claims, and organize the reasons and evidence logically.
	   Informational. Introduce a topic clearly, previewing what is to follow; organize ideas, concepts, and information, using strategies such as definition, classification, comparison/contrast, and cause/effect; include formatting (e.g., headings), graphics (e.g., charts, tables), and multimedia when useful to aiding comprehension.
		Reading Standards for Informational Text Analyze in detail the structure of a specific paragraph in a text, including the role of particular sentences in developing and refining a key concept.
		
		Writing Standards *Argumentative.* Introduce claim(s), acknowledge and distinguish the claim(s) from alternate or opposing claims, and organize the reasons and evidence logically.
		   Informational. Write informative/ explanatory texts to examine a topic and convey ideas, concepts, and information through the selection, organization, and analysis of relevant content.
			Reading Standards for Informational Text Analyze in detail how an author's ideas or claims are developed and refined by particular sentences, paragraphs, or larger portions of a text (e.g., a section or chapter).
			
			Writing Standards *Argumentative.* Introduce precise claim(s), distinguish the claim(s) from alternate or opposing claims, and create an organization that establishes clear relationships among claim(s), counterclaims, reasons, and evidence.
			   Informational. Write informative/ explanatory texts to examine and convey complex ideas, concepts, and information clearly and accurately through the effective selection, organization, and analysis of content.

Conclusion

Text structure is a tool for reading and writing vital to the language arts tool-box. It is time to take some action . . .

Action Steps

1. Design a pretest to help identify what your students already know about common text structures (I suggest finding five different paragraphs, each modeling a different structure. Then, have students identify the text structure in use). After administering this pretest, report: Which text structures do they know? Which ones do you need to teach in more depth?

   _____

   _____

   _____

   _____

2. Make a plan for teaching the remaining text structures. How will you help students become adept at basic identification?

   _____

   _____

   _____

   _____

3. Have students bring in an article from the local paper. Model the use of the Text Structure Think-Mat with an article of your own. Then, have students use the Think-Mat to identify the text structure of the article they brought in.

   Did the Think-Mat help them in their quest? How can you tell?

   _____

   _____

   _____

   _____

4. Finally, it is time to scaffold some writing. Do your students need to use copy change to get them started or are they ready to use the Think-Mat

to write longer pieces? Create a plan of action to implement either (or both!) writing ideas.

_____

_____

_____

_____

Works Cited

Bintz, W., Wright, P., & Sheffer, J. (2010). Using copy change with tradebooks to teach Earth science. *The Reading Teacher, 64*, 106–119.

Brown, M. W. (1949). *The important book.* New York: HarperCollins.

Dreher, M., & Gray, J. (2009). Compare, contrast, comprehend: Using compare-contrast text structures with ELLs in K-3 classrooms. *The Reading Teacher, 63*, 132–141.

Dymock, S., & Nicholson, T. (2010). "High five!" Strategies to increase comprehension of expository text. *The Reading Teacher, 64*, 166–178.

Foreman, M. (2011). *Fortunately, unfortunately.* London: Andersen Press.

Gaddy, S., Bakken, J., & Fulk, B. (2008). The effects of teaching text-structure strategies to postsecondary students with learning disabilities to improve their reading comprehension on expository science text passages. *Journal of Postsecondary Education and Disability, 20*, 100–119.

Li-Hao, Y., Schwartz, A., & Baule, A. (2011). The impact of text-structure strategy instruction on the text recall and eye-movement patterns of second language English readers. *Reading Psychology, 32*, 495–511.

Meyer, B., & Rice, G. (1984). The structure of text. In P. Pearson, R. Barr, M. Kamil, & P. Mosenthal (Eds.), *Handbook of reading research* (pp. 319–351). New York: Longman.

National Governors Association for Best Practices, Council of Chief State School Officers. (2011). Common core state standards (English language arts). Washington, DC: Author.

Numeroff, L. (2010). *If you give a mouse a cookie.* NY: Harper Collins.

Rasinski, T., & Padak, N. (2000). *Effective reading strategies* (2nd ed.) Upper Saddle River, NJ: Prentice Hall.

Read, S., Reutzel, D., & Fawson, P. (2008). Do you want to know what I learned? Using informational trade books as models to teach text structure. *Early Childhood Education, 36*, 213–219.

Shanahan, T., Fisher, D., & Frey, N. (2012). The challenge of challenging text. *Educational Leadership, 69*, 58–62.

Wiggins, G., & McTighe, J. (2005). *Understanding by design* (2nd ed.) New York: Pearson.

Template 8.1 Text Structure Chart

Text Structure	Associated Graphic Organizer	Signal Words
Descriptive		No specific signal words
Sequence		first next second until third while last soon then after at that time now during immediately finally
Compare/Contrast	Name 1 Name 2 Attribute 1 Attribute 2 Attribute 3	however even though but on the contrary yet otherwise despite in comparion still on the other hand
Cause & Effect	Cause / Effect / Effect / Effect	for this reason thus in order to as a result because consequently so that on account of therefore accordingly
Problem/Solution	Problem / Attempted Solutions Who 1. What When 2. Where Why Results	problem solution because cause since as a result so that

Copyright 2014 Taylor & Francis. All rights reserved. www.routledge.com

Template 8.2   Fortunately, Unfortunately Copy Change Template

Name_____

Fortunately . . .

Explain the cause and effect of events using the space below. Fortunately will be the cause and unfortunately will be the effect.

Fortunately, _____

_____

But unfortunately,

_____

_____

Fortunately, _____

_____

But unfortunately,

_____

_____

Fortunately, _____

_____

But unfortunately,

_____

_____

Copyright 2014 Taylor & Francis. All rights reserved. www.routledge.com

Template 8.3   Text Structure Think-Mat

Descriptive	Text Structure Think-Mat	Sequence/Chronological
Fact — Fact — Central idea — Fact — Fact		First → Second → Third [Text]

Compare/Contrast	Cause/Effect	Problem/Solution

Compare/Contrast

	Name 1	Name 2
Attribute 1		
Attribute 2		
Attribute 3		

Cause/Effect

Cause → Effect / Effect / Effect

Problem/Solution

Problem	Attempted Solutions
Who What	1.
When	2.
Where Why	
Results	

Copyright 2014 Taylor & Francis. All rights reserved. www.routledge.com

Encourage Independent Reading of Nonfiction Texts as Part of a Balanced Self-Selected Reading Diet

On each student's desk was a stack of the books they have read all year. The administrative team walked around, chatting with students about their choices, enjoying their enthusiastic responses as they described favorite books, authors, and plans for summer reading. I stopped in front of Casey, a project of mine since I had been his Title I Reading teacher many years ago when he was in elementary school. His face was not happy. "Casey," I said, kneeling by his desk, "why the frown?" He crossed his arms and looked up at me. "I read a lot this year, Mrs. W., I swear! But the teacher said sports books didn't count, so I only have these," waving his hand towards the two classics on his desk. "These were the ones we read together."

Why Is This Item on the List So Important?

Casey perfectly exemplifies why encouraging nonfiction reading during independent reading is so important; for reluctant or struggling readers, informational text is often the best way to lure them onto the lifelong reading path (Kelsey, 2011). Casey was a sports nut. Present him with a biography on a sports figure or a stats book, and he was happily engaged for hours. Force anything historical or science fiction on him, and he would choke down a page before doing a really great job at faking reading (you know exactly what I mean: turning a page every now and then, bent over the book with full absorption. But ask him what happened and you would get an empty smile).

And yet, there is a nonfiction "desert" in many language arts classroom (Parsons, 2012). Classroom and school libraries are falling short when it comes to providing access to nonfiction as arresting as the fiction books that usually attract us language arts teachers. Think about the last great book you read for fun—chances are this book was a fiction text, the latest best-seller, perhaps. But our preferences, while influential on our students, may not match up to their likes and dislikes.

There is hidden potential in nonfiction books for struggling readers (Dreher, 2010). We can book talk popular books like *The Hunger Games, Divergent,* and *Life as We Knew It* as much as we want (some of my personal favorite young adult books), but it is books like *Bomb: The Race to Build—and Steal—the World's Most Dangerous Weapon* and *How They Croaked: The Awful Ends of the Awfully Famous* that might make readers out of non-readers!

> **Do this—not that principle #9: DO encourage independent reading of nonfiction texts as part of a balanced self-selected reading diet; DON'T read nonfiction texts only in whole group settings.**

To Get Started

Despite the mixed messages out there, the value of independent reading cannot be dismissed. Encouraging independent reading as part of the language arts reading curriculum will help build the "proficiency" students need to meet the demands of complex texts, as cited in Standard 10 under both Reading Literary Text and Reading Informational Text (CCSS, 2011). Only reading whole class texts, under the guidance of the teacher, or only reading texts in small, supported groups will not get students to a point of independence and application in the critical skills students must possess to analyze and discuss all texts with confidence.

I know there are teachers who worry that an independent reading component is not true "teaching," that an administrator will walk in and see a roomful of students bent over their books and the teacher will be evaluated poorly for lack of instruction. This paradigm must shift. Giving the students the accessibility to great books and the time to read can be some of the best teaching we can do (Atwell, 2007). Guiding readers through a text is one thing, allowing students choice in reading material and space and time to practice reading at their success level is taking our goal as teachers very seriously—we have to see if they can do the same kind of work that we do in guided reading with texts by themselves.

Clarifying the difference between D.E.A.R. (Drop Everything and Read) or S.S.R. (Self-Selected Reading) and independent reading can be a helpful way to make the case for independent reading in your classroom. Table 9.1 highlights these differences.

Table 9.1   The Difference Between DEAR/SSR and Independent Reading

D.E.A.R./S.S.R.	Independent Reading
◆ Choice in text selection is honored	◆ Choice in text selection is honored *within the student's successful reading level*; type of text may be given (fiction or nonfiction)
◆ Accountability is minimal—books are read to be celebrated and shared	◆ Accountability is high; students show they are able to apply skills and strategies to what they are reading
◆ Read aloud done to begin or end this time is for entertainment, exposure, and encouragement	◆ Read aloud done to begin this time is done to model thinking with texts
◆ A time for escape, relaxation, and enjoyment with texts	◆ A time for enjoyment with a text, but with an intention set for reading

Routman, 2003

There is a place for both types of reading in the Common Core classroom. Both types of reading encourage students to create a lifelong reading identity, making reading personal, relevant, and useful (Hinchman, Alvermann, Boyd, Brozo, & Vacca, 2003/2004; Young, Moss, & Cornwell, 2007). And if you are still not convinced, consider this: An increase in reading, spelling, vocabulary, and writing skills are payoffs for students who have opportunities to engage in sustained, independent reading practice (Beck, McKeown & Kucan, 2002; Krashen, 2004; Young, Moss, & Cornwell 2007).

Updated Strategy #1: Using the Pyramid Approach to Encourage Nonfiction, Self-Selected Reading

The Readers' Workshop approach to language arts instruction is well-documented (Atwell, 2007; Calkins, Ehrenworth, & Lehman, 2012; Fountas & Pinnell, 2002). The workshop approach includes:

♦ A minilesson (15–20 minutes) where the teacher models and guides practice in a particular skill or strategy for the whole class or a small group in a variety of purposeful texts.

♦ The minilesson is followed by independent reading. Students choose texts at their success level (95% of words read successfully). Students record reactions to the text and apply the minilesson to their self-selected text.

♦ Teachers confer with students on a regular basis to ensure successful application of the minilesson, appropriate text selection, and comprehension.

♦ More recently, after a set amount of a time, teachers give a short pre/post assessment to gauge student progress on the standard, helping them to structure minilessons, conferences, and guided work as appropriate.

An updated approach to the Readers' Workshop is giving the nonfiction standards equal or even weighted billing in the minilessons, assessments, and texts read during workshop time. Traditionally, workshop time focused on fiction elements, asking students to find theme, trace plot, and analyze mood in the texts that they read. Readers' Workshop honors choice and, in most cases, the choices that students made in self-selected reading texts were fiction. But this might actually not mirror student choice: Goodwin and Miller (2012) report that using nonfiction in the language arts classroom taps into student interests unlike many fiction texts. Think about it: Our reluctant readers may not be into vampires, post-apocalyptic societies, or dystopias, but they may be interested in gaming, sports, cooking, or history. A balanced diet approach to Readers' Workshop might help lure them in; they still get choice, but their choices are broadened to include fiction or nonfiction.

I am calling this type of Readers' Workshop the "Pyramid Approach" after an article I read in a library journal (Failmezger, 2006). The author advocated making nonfiction the base of all reading, the type of reading we ask students to do the most, long before the Common Core State Standards was released. Failmezger felt that nonfiction reading prepared our students for a variety of literacy tasks and urged teachers and librarians to make nonfiction a bigger part of our reading diets. If we take this approach during Readers' Workshop, we would have to be slightly more directive in the choices we gave students; for a certain length of time, teachers would ask students to select fiction or nonfiction texts, depending on the type of standards we would be teaching in our minilessons. Figure 9.1 presents an adapted Pyramid Approach to student reading.

Figure 9.1   The Pyramid Approach to Self-Selected Reading

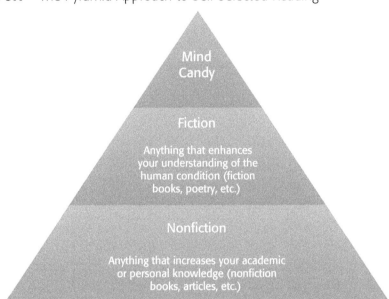

Adapted from Failmezger, 2006

To make this even clearer to students, you could put numbers or specific types of each reading paired with this pyramid to give them a goal to reach for in working this type of balanced approach. This calls to mind Donnalynn Miller's 40 book challenge, from *The Book Whisperer* (2009): She, too, advocates for a balanced reading diet, giving students a sort of reading roadmap to help them read a variety of books during her independent reading time.

Differentiation. The key to differentiation in a Pyramid Approach to teaching the standards lies with each student's selection of texts to use during the independent reading/application portion of the workshop. It is an instructional approach that I like to call "naturally differentiated;" we rely on students' knowledge of their own reading strengths and challenges to choose books that they can read with success. Many teachers who teach in a workshop approach spend the first few weeks of school doing a variety of assessments, reading inventories, and surveys to see where their students are starting the year and then conferring with students to be clear about each student's reading goals (Atwell, 2007; Miller, 2009). Teachers then need to reassess and confer with students regularly to ensure they are choosing books that fit into the "just right" category that ensures students will continue to grow (Miller, 2009).

Many middle and high school teachers dismiss a workshop approach because it differs so greatly from the traditional "one book-one class" instructional approach that many of us experienced ourselves. But a workshop's abilities to teach and meet standards while providing a way to ease differentiation into the curriculum is unprecedented and even the most reluctant teachers have found success with devoting just a portion of their language arts block to this type of instruction (Morgan & Wagner, 2013).

Updated Strategy #2: Creating a Common Core
Aligned Classroom Library

Teachers need to evaluate their classroom libraries to see if they meet the nonfiction reading needs of all of our students. The International Reading Association (1999) recommends that a good classroom library has at least seven books per student and then suggests adding two to three titles per student over the course of the year. A colleague of mine, with a truly extensive classroom library, recently went through and categorized her books to see if she was providing a balance in her library. She knew the answer before we even began; she was lacking nonfiction, a reflection of her own reading preferences that she was unknowingly passing on to her students.

To meet students' reading levels and interests, books representing a variety of nonfiction topics need to be in your library. And you shouldn't stop at books! Think about the type of reading you do as an adult—we read the news (online and in traditional paper formats), magazines for entertainment and knowledge, recipes, and manuals to navigate life, to the tune of 90% of our reading (Maloch & Horsey, 2013). A true 21st-century classroom library might include daily, weekly, and monthly subscriptions (both Internet and paper-based), e-book formats where students can download and read materials on personal and shared devices, and traditional books. A student can read and write about an author's point of view in a newspaper article as well as they can in a biography in book form. Our students have already adapted to this; as teachers, it is time to make the shift. Table 9.2 provides a list of elements a language arts teacher might look for as they shift their classroom library to meet the nonfiction needs of the Common Core State Standards.

Table 9.2 Elements of a Common Core-based Classroom Library

Elements	Needs Work	Meets It!
At least 50% of the texts are nonfiction		
A selection of biographies and autobiographies at a variety of levels are present		
Periodicals are available for daily/weekly use during independent reading		
Other informational texts are available at a variety of levels and on a variety of topics		
Fiction in a variety of formats is represented (historical, science, fantasy, contemporary realistic)		
Poetry is present in the library		

The most common question I get about encouraging students to read more nonfiction is "Where do I find good nonfiction books and periodicals?" The first place I look to find good nonfiction texts are the award winners; Table 9.3 gives a listing and descriptions of nonfiction awards for children's and young adult literature.

Table 9.3 Children's and Young Adult Award Winning Nonfiction Literature

Award	Description
International Reading Association (IRA)—Children's and Young Adult Book Awards	♦ This award is given to the best new book published in fiction and nonfiction each year. ♦ www.reading.org/Resources/ AwardsandGrants/childrens_ira.aspx
Young Adult Library Services Association (YALSA)—Award for Excellence in Nonfiction for Young Adults	♦ This award honors the best nonfiction book published for young adults (ages 12–18) each year. ♦ www.ala.org/yalsa/nonfiction
National Council of Teachers of English (NCTE)—Orbis Pictus Award for Outstanding Nonfiction for Children	♦ This award promotes and recognizes excellence in the writing of nonfiction for children. ♦ www.ncte.org/awards/orbispictus

I also have a few "go to" periodicals for children and young adults (see Table 9.4).

Table 9.4 Children's and Young Adult Nonfiction Periodicals

Periodical	Description
Time for Kids	Version of the adult magazine *Time*. Current events, recognition of historical events of significance, even kid-written articles! Paper version published monthly; Internet content is updated weekly.
	Differentiated versions available based on grade level.
	www.timeforkids.com
National Geographic Kids	Version of the adult magazine *National Geographic*. Great for social studies and science connections. Paper version published monthly; Internet content updated daily.
	http://kids.nationalgeographic.com/kids/
Sports Illustrated Kids	Version of the adult magazine *Sports Illustrated*. Hook for our sports-minded readers! Paper version published monthly; Internet content updated weekly.
	www.sikids.com
Ranger Rick	Published by the National Wildlife Fund. Great science content; amazing photos! Published monthly; Internet content updated weekly.
	www.nwf.org/kids/ranger-rick.aspx

The final point to consider when encouraging nonfiction text selection for independent reading is modeling your own reading of these types of texts. As I stated above, I am more of a fiction fan than a nonfiction reader when it comes to books. Every once in a while, I happen upon a great nonfiction book, like *Unbroken*, by Laura Hillenbrand, and read it cover to cover as fast as I can. But I realized that my reading habits were not setting the right example for my students. My preservice teachers and I use a website called Shelfari (www.shelfari.com) to share our reading (it's like Facebook for books!). I had a student point out that the majority of the books on my virtual "shelf" were historical and contemporary realistic fiction, mostly with female protagonists. And they were absolutely right. Realizing that my students were not only getting book recommendations from my reading but also monitoring if I was "walking the walk" made me be more intentional in my personal reading.

Common Core Connection

The strategies presented above fit well with a variety of standards in the Common Core State Standards for English Language Arts (see Figure 9.2).

However, like Chapter 3, one main standard is addressed by the simple idea of encouraging students to read more nonfiction as part of independent reading in the language arts curriculum.

Figure 9.2 Common Core State Standards Addressed in This Chapter

Grade Level	**4–10**
Standard Addressed	**Reading Standards for Informational Text** By the end of the year, read and comprehend informational texts.

Conclusion

Balancing your reading diet with nonfiction is like balancing your plate with vegetables and fruit: it's good for you, you know you should do it, but it can be hard to take that first step. It's time to take that first step together through some action . . .

Action Steps

1. Take a look at your personal reading preferences: Are you a nonfiction reader, yourself? Take an inventory of your reading from the past three months, using the space below.

   Fiction books:

   Nonfiction books:

   Magazines:

   Other:

   Do you have a balanced reading life? If not, what will you do to be a better role model for your students?

   _____

   _____

   _____

   _____

2. Using Table 9.2, take an inventory of your classroom library. Does it meet the requirements recommended for meeting the Common Core? If not, what can you do to boost your nonfiction holdings?

_____

_____

_____

_____

3. How can you see a Readers' Workshop model fitting into your classroom?

_____

_____

_____

_____

Works Cited

Atwell, N. (2007). *The reading zone: How to help kids become skilled, passionate, habitual, critical readers.* New York: Scholastic.

Beck, I., McKeown, M., & Kucan, L. (2002). *Bringing words to life: Robust vocabulary instruction.* New York: Guilford.

Calkins, L., Ehrenworth, M., & Lehman, C. (2012). *Pathways to the Common Core: Accelerating achievement.* Portsmouth, NH: Heinemann.

Dreher, M. (2010). Motivating struggling readers by tapping the potential of information books. *Reading & Writing Quarterly, 19,* 25–38.

Failmezger, T. (2006). Feed your brain! *Library Media Connection,* 22–23.

Fountas, I., & Pinnell, G. (2002). *Guiding readers and writers (grades 3–6): Teaching comprehension, genre, and content literacy.* Portsmouth, NH: Heinemann.

Goodwin, B., & Miller, K. (2012). Nonfiction reading promotes student success. *Educational Leadership, 70,* 80–82.

Hinchman, K., Alvermann, D., Boyd, F., Brozo, W., & Vacca, R. (2003/2004). Supporting older students' in- and out-of-school literacies. *Journal of Adolescent & Adult Literacy, 47,* 304–310.

International Reading Association. (1999). *Classroom and school library position statement.* Newark, DE: International Reading Association.

Kelsey, M. (2011). Compelling students to read with compelling nonfiction. *Knowledge Quest, 39,* 35–39.

Krashen, S. (2004). *The power of reading: Insights from the research.* New York: Libraries Unlimited.

Maloch, B., & Horsey, M. (2013). Living inquiry: Learning from and about informational texts in a second-grade classroom. *The Reading Teacher, 66,* 475–485.

Miller, D. (2009). *The book whisperer: Awakening the inner reader in every child.* New York: Jossey-Bass.

Morgan, D., & Wagner, C. (2013). "What's the catch?" Providing reading choice in a high school classroom. *Journal of Adolescent and Adult Literacy, 56,* 659–667.

National Governors Association for Best Practices, Council of Chief State School Officers. (2011). Common core state standards (English language arts). Washington, DC: Author.

Parsons, C. (2012). Making nonfiction accessible for young readers. *Reading Today, 30,* 21–23.

Routman, R. (2003). *Reading essentials: The specifics you need to teach reading well.* Portsmouth, NH: Heinemann.

Young, T., Moss, B., & Cornwell, L. (2007). The classroom library: A place for nonfiction, nonfiction in its place. *Reading Horizons, 48,* 1–18.

Chapter 10

Use Nonfiction for Active Comprehension Strategies Like Readers' Theatre, Tableaux, and Character Walks

The students sat at their desks, facing the teacher at the front, who had an article about the Civil Rights Movement on the Elmo. Body language was bored: slumped backs, hands holding up heads, eyelids drooping. Even though students had copies of the article themselves, only a few were actually holding them in their hands. After reading through it, the teacher announced it was time to get back into groups to continue discussing the class book, The Watsons Go to Birmingham. Suddenly, it was like a new group of students sat in front of me: students were leaning in to share ideas and books were grasped in hands. When they left, before I could even comment, the teacher said, "I know; they love their fiction. I wish I could get them to like the nonfiction we are pairing with the text as much as they like the book."

Why Is This Item on the List So Important?

The power we have as teachers is frightening. I can admit that I am not a Twain fan, and when my English department head announced that all eighth grade teachers must teach *The Adventures of Huckleberry Finn*, I complained with the best of them. I then walked into class the next day and proclaimed with a defeatist attitude: "Okay, you guys, we have to read this book because the school says so. I don't like it very much, but we will get through it somehow." As you can imagine, the students took their cue from me and moaned and groaned their way through a poorly designed unit that I threw together at the last minute.

The teacher referenced in the anecdote above didn't realize it, but by using discussion and creativity in conjunction with the fiction text in the classroom, she was "blessing" the book with active, engaged reading strategies. I found out over the course of a few weeks of observations and coaching that anytime she used a nonfiction text, she used the same routine: A photocopied article that students couldn't write on, lights off so she could use the Elmo, and almost an entire repertoire of teacher-centered instruction. She was subconsciously giving off two messages about her nonfiction texts: "You (the students) can't handle these, so I will tell you all you need to know" and "Nonfiction is boring." When I gently pointed this out to her, she first protested, then thought about it, and then put her hand over her mouth in shock. "I'm not much for nonfiction," she admitted. "I am showing that through my teaching, aren't I?"

> **Do this—not that principle #10: DO use nonfiction for active comprehension strategies like Readers' Theatre, Tableaux and Character Walks. DON'T make nonfiction reading a passive, seated experience only.**

To Get Started

The easiest way to be honest with yourself about your nonfiction teaching strategies is to look back at a lesson plan book from a previous year. If you used nonfiction, what kind of instruction was planned? Chances are the instruction was teacher-centered, student-passive instruction (Guthrie et al., 2006; Ivey & Broaddus, 2000). How can we explain this phenomenon? Many teachers feel that nonfiction text is harder than fiction text and therefore must be more explicitly taught (Duke, 2004). Others feel that nonfiction is dry and hard to "liven up" with engaging strategies (Duke, 2004; Harvey & Goudis, 2007). And, like the teacher above, a final group simply dislikes nonfiction and teaches it with a "clean out the litter box" demeanor.

We have dispelled the myths from above throughout this book. Nonfiction text can be differentiated (Chapter 3). Nonfiction text can be interesting and engaging (Chapters 1 & 9). This final chapter is dedicated to three strategies that move beyond a docile reading experience to one filled with interaction, movement, and expression. Clean out some of the "dry" teaching you have done in conjunction with nonfiction text in the past and try out any or all of the three active comprehension strategies described below:

Updated Strategy #1: Using Readers' Theatre with Nonfiction Text

Readers' Theatre is a during or post reading strategy that helps students make a text come alive (Clementi, 2010; Keehn, Harmon, & Shoho, 2008). Based on radio plays from the 1930s, students have nothing but their voices to breathe life and enthusiasm into a text. Figure 10.1 shows the difference between Readers' Theatre and a play. Payoffs from Readers' Theatre can be powerful—student comprehension, fluency, inference, and summarizing skills can all be positively affected by the use of the strategy (Keehn, 2003; Young & Rasinski, 2009).

Figure 10.1 The Difference Between Readers' Theatre and a Play

Readers' Theatre	Play
Limited physical movement	Movements/ Staging
No backdrop	Props
Limited props	Scenery
No memorization	Memorization

During reading. As a during reading strategy, Readers' Theatre becomes the informational text, itself. Pass out the script, divide up roles, and read! Readers' Theatre in this form is an excellent replacement for Round Robin Reading, the scourge of read aloud by students everywhere (Opitz & Rasinski, 2008). A Readers' Theatre script provides authenticity in dividing up the read aloud, forcing students to pay attention to everything being read by their peers and not just picking a paragraph, practicing it again and again, and waiting nervously for their turn.

There are amazing prepared scripts available for free on the Internet and for purchase on nonfiction topics. They are a great way to introduce the idea of Readers' Theatre to students, showing them the power of shared performance when learning about new topics. An example of this came in a course I teach every fall, Reading and Writing in Middle Childhood Education. We had a day to delve into Readers' Theatre, and I brought in prepared scripts on a variety of topics. One script was about The Christmas Truce (Shepherd, 2001). This event during World War I happened on a Christmas Eve, when soldiers crossed enemy lines to share the holiday together. The story is told through letters home by the soldiers. A group of students read the script to the class, and, by the end of the reading, there was not a dry eye in the house. Table 10.1 gives a short list of resources of places to find great nonfiction Readers' Theatre scripts.

Table 10.1   Resources for Readers' Theatre scripts

1. Aaron Shepard's RT Page: www.aaronshep.com/rt/
2. Dr. Young's Reading Room: www.thebestclass.org/rtscripts.html
3. Read Write Think: www.readwritethink.org/classroom-resources/ lesson-plans/readers-theatre-172.html (actually a lesson plan to write RT!)

Postreading. As a postreading strategy, Readers' Theatre becomes both a comprehension and response strategy, as well as an advanced writing activity. Students read a text in its traditional format and then turn it into a Readers' Theatre script. This transformation hits at so many skills: main idea, details, summary, bias, author's purpose—to write a Readers' Theatre script, students have to go back to the source material again and again. It is close reading without calling it close reading!

To have students prepare their own scripts, it is advisable to first have them read and analyze characteristics of prepared scripts. From there, I walk students through a series of steps:

♦ Read a text several times. Brainstorm a list of possible roles: Characters, narrator(s), even a sound effect person, if necessary!

♦ Discuss the difference between narrators and characters (did we just hit a Reading, Literary Text Standard while analyzing an informational text?). I summarize this for students by saying that narrators say what is outside the quotation marks in a text while characters say what is inside the quotation marks. If a text is a pure descriptive text (text structure analysis!), then students may want to create dialogue.

♦ Using a shared word processing program, like GoogleDoc, allows students to work in groups to actually write their script. Make sure that examples of Readers' Theatre format abound to ensure the final product looks like a Readers' Theatre script.

♦ Perform! One of the joys of this strategy is having different groups of students turn the same text into Readers' Theatre scripts; it is fascinating to see how each group treats the topic.

It is even possible to up the rigor with this strategy. I first choose informational texts that include dialogue or have obvious characters for transformation into a Readers' Theatre script. From there, I choose more opaque texts, like encyclopedia entries, to challenge students' inference skills. The ultimate challenge is to present students with several texts on the same topic and to have them integrate these resources into a single, cohesive, Readers' Theatre script.

Updated Strategy #2: Using Tableaux to Aid Comprehension with Nonfiction Text

Tableaux is an active reading, whole group strategy to be used to focus student attention during the reading of a text or after reading to deepen comprehension and promote inferences. Best described as "still charades" (Wilfong, 2012), it allows students to show their visualization of an event or idea from the text by getting their whole body involved (Rasinski, 2003; Tortello, 2004; Wilhelm, 2002). To implement this strategy, follow these steps:

- ♦ To introduce the strategy, select a text with clear events. A sequence/ chronological text will best support the initial teaching of the strategy.

- ♦ Identify five to seven events from the text that are key to comprehension.

- ♦ Write each event on a notecard. You can either summarize the event or copy the exact sentence or two that captures the event. Figure 10.2 has a sample article and event sequence that could be used with the Tableaux strategy.

- ♦ Divide students into groups of four or five. Give each group a notecard. Tell students that they will use their bodies to create a still picture of the event—no talking or movement allowed! Depending on how many "characters" are necessary for their event or scene, additional students in the group can be scenery or props. Five minutes is more than enough time for them to create their scene.

- ♦ Call groups to the front of the room to recreate their scene or event for the rest of the class without telling them which scene they were assigned. I usually count back from three and then announce, "Strike a pose!"

- ♦ Give the class a few moments to ponder the scene in front of them. Then, allow students to guess which scene is being depicted. If students are stumped, ask them which student in the scene they would like interviewed to get a clue about what is going on. I tap that student, and then he or she gets to infer for us. I ask, "Who are you and what is going on right now?" The student responds with his or her title and a description from that character's (or prop's!) point of view. If necessary, I tap another student to help clarify the situation.

♦ Once students have guessed the scene being portrayed, we move onto the next one.

Figure 10.2   Article and Event Sequence to Use with Tableaux

A crowd of visitors at Brookfield Zoo looked on in horror Friday afternoon as they watched a toddler tumble more than 15 feet in a pit, landing near seven gorillas.

But as zoo patrons cried out for help, expecting the worst for the 3-year-old boy lying battered on the concrete below, an unlikely hero emerged.

A female ape, with her own baby clinging to her back, lumbered over to the boy, cradled him in arms, carried him to a doorway and laid him gingerly at the feet of waiting paramedics.

Zoo spokesperson Sondra Catzen said Binti Jua, a rare western lowland gorilla who has received training on how to be a good mother, appeared to act "out of purely maternalistic compassion for the human child."

"She picked up the boy, kind of cradling him, and walked him around," said Catzen.

"Another gorilla walked toward the boy, and she kind of turned around and walked away from the other gorillas and tried to be protective," said Carrie Stewart, a zoo visitor who witnessed the incident.

At first it appeared the boy had been knocked unconscious by the fall, witnesses told zoo officials. But "He was alert and crying when the paramedics came and got him," Catzen said.

Excerpt from the *Chicago Tribune*, in Raphael & Au (2002, p. 18)

Updated Strategy #3: Using Character Walks to Infer about Nonfiction Text Topics

The final active comprehension strategy comes from Jeff Wilhelm, the genius behind the Tea Party strategy described in Chapter 1. Character walks are a true during reading strategy; they are used while reading to draw student attention to a problem or interesting idea in a text before reading to see how the problem is solved or how the idea plays out (Wilhelm, 2002). Like Tableaux above, this strategy gets students out of their seats and talking about text. It does not take long but provides that brain break many students need while reading. To implement it in your classroom, follow these steps:

♦ Select a problem/solution or cause/effect text to use in conjunction with this strategy. Read to identify a logical stopping point in the middle of the text.

♦ Have students read to this point in the text.

♦ Invite students to stand up and form two concentric circles in the room (Yes, this requires a bit of space. I've been known to take students out into the hallway so that we don't have to move furniture.)

♦ Explain to students that they will be assuming the role of an important idea or figure in the text. For example, if you had read an article about the food chain, the inside circle could be a lion (the top of the food chain), while the outside circle could be an antelope that the lion wishes to eat.

♦ Have students walk in their respective circles; counterclockwise for the inner circle and clockwise for the outer circle.

♦ At your signal, have students stop opposite someone from the other circle. Tell the inner circle they have 30 seconds to explain to their counterpart their point of view on the text. Using the lion/antelope example, the lions could explain to the antelopes why it was the rules of nature for them to wish to eat them.

♦ Allow the outer circle to respond to this dialogue from their partner. The antelope circle could reply to the lion about why it would benefit the lion to wait for meatier, tastier prey.

♦ On your signal again, have circles continue walking, stop with a new partner, and repeat the cycle, with new prompts to help them infer about the text.

With this strategy, it is imperative to have good prompts for student response. It can also be used to craft the use of textual evidence in responses; students could be asked to not only infer as if they were the character or figure from the text in their dialogue with their partner but also provide textual evidence to support their inferences!

Common Core Connection

The strategies presented above fit well with a variety of standards in the Common Core State Standards for English Language Arts (see Figure 10.3).

Figure 10.3 Common Core State Standards Addressed in This Chapter

Grade Level	4	5	6
Standard Addressed	**Reading Standards for Informational Text** Refer to details and examples in a text when explaining what the text says explicitly and when drawing inferences from the text. Explain events, procedures, ideas, or concepts in a historical, scientific, or technical text, including what happened and why, based on specific information in the text. By the end of the year, read and comprehend informational texts.	**Reading Standards for Informational Text** Quote accurately when explaining what the text says explicitly and when drawing inferences. Explain the relationships or interactions between two or more individuals, events, ideas or concepts in a historical, scientific, or technical text based on specific information in the text. By the end of the year, read and comprehend informational texts.	**Reading Standards for Informational Text** Cite textual evidence to support analysis of what the text says explicitly as well as inferences drawn from the text. Analyze in detail how a key individual, event, or idea is introduced, illustrated, and elaborated in a text (e.g., through examples or anecdotes). By the end of the year, read and comprehend informational texts.

Grade Level	7	8	9–10
Standard Addressed	**Reading Standards for Informational Text** Cite several pieces of textual evidence to support analysis of what the text says explicitly as well as inferences drawn from the text. By the end of the year, read and comprehend informational texts.	**Reading Standards for Informational Text** Cite several pieces of textual evidence to support analysis of what the text says explicitly as well as inferences drawn from the text. By the end of the year, read and comprehend informational texts.	**Reading Standards for Informational Text** Cite strong and thorough textual evidence to support analysis of what the text says explicitly as well as inferences drawn from the text. Analyze how the author unfolds an analysis or series of events, including the order in which the points are made, how they are introduced and developed, and the connections drawn between them. By the end of the year, read and comprehend informational texts.

Conclusion

Reading informational text in the language arts classroom does not have to be a boring, dry endeavor! It is time to take some action . . .

Action Step

1. Which of the three strategies presented in this chapter are you most drawn to? Why?

_____

_____

_____

Works Cited

Clementi, L. B. (2010). Readers Theater. *Phi Delta Kappan, 91*(5), 85–88.

Duke, N. (2004). The case for informational text. *Educational Leadership, 61*, 40–44.

Guthrie, J., Wigfield, A., Humenick, N., Perencevich, K., Taboada, A., & Barbosa, P. (2006). Influences of stimulating tasks on reading motivation and comprehension. *The Journal of Educational Research, 99*, 232–246.

Harvey, S., & Goudis, A. (2007). *Strategies that work: Teaching comprehension for understanding and engagement.* Portland, ME: Stenhouse.

Ivey, G., & Broaddus, K. (2000). Tailoring the fit: Reading instruction and middle school students. *The Reading Teacher, 54*, 68–78.

Keehn, S. (2003). The effect of instruction and practice through Readers Theatre on young readers' oral reading fluency. *Literacy Research and Instruction, 42*, 40–61.

Keehn, S., Harmon, J., & Shoho, A. (2008). Issues of fluency, comprehension, and vocabulary. *Reading and Writing Quarterly, 24*, 335–362.

Opitz, M., & Rasinski, T. (2008). *Goodbye round robin reading.* Portsmouth, NH: Heinemann.

Raphael, T., & Au, K. (2002). *Super QAR for testwise students.* Columbus, OH: McGraw Hill.

Rasinski, T. (2003). *The fluent reader: Oral reading strategies for building word recognition, fluency, and comprehension.* New York: Scholastic.

Shepherd, A. (2001). The Christmas Truce. Retrieved November 1, 2013, from www.aaronshep.com/rt/RTE34.html

Tortello, R. (2004). Tableaux vivants in the literature classroom. *The Reading Teacher, 58*, 206–208.

Wilfong, L. (2012). *Vocabulary strategies that work: Do this—not that!* New York: Routledge.

Wilhelm, J. (2002). *Action strategies for deepening comprehension: Using drama strategies to assist reading performance.* New York: Scholastic.

Young, C., & Rasinski, T. (2009). Implementing Readers Theatre as an approach to classroom fluency instruction. *The Reading Teacher, 63*, 4–13.

www.ingramcontent.com/pod-product-compliance
Ingram Content Group UK Ltd.
Pitfield, Milton Keynes, MK11 3LW, UK
UKHW010022280225
455677UK00023B/751